MW01116288

THE
SHADOW WORK
WORKBOOK

A Transformative Self-Care Journey to Heal Past Traumas, Awaken Your Inner Child, and Uncover Your Authentic Self with Empowering Exercises & Prompts

Scarlett Kent

Your support is important to me!

Great things can start from a small gesture!

Leave a sincere review to support my work.

This would help to share and find this knowledge more easily to people who are looking for it.

© Copyright 2023 by Scarlett Kent - All right reserved.

No parts of the book may be reproduced in any form without permission from the author.
Written by Scarlett Kent.
First Edition, First print, 2023

Copyright notice

This statement is legally binding as deemed by the Committee of Publishers Association and the American Bar Association for the territory of the United States. Other jurisdictions may apply their own legal statutes. Any reproduction, transmission, or copying of this material contained in this work without the express written consent of the copyright holder shall be deemed as a copyright violation as per the current legislation in force on the date of publishing and the subsequent time thereafter. All additional works derived from this material may be claimed by the holder of this copyright.

Limited Liability

This book is only for personal use. Please note the information contained within this document is for educational and entertainment purposes only and no warranties of any kind are declared or implied. Readers acknowledge that the author is not engaging in the rendering of professional and other types of advice. While the author has gone to every extent to furnish up-to-date and true information, no claims can be made as to its accuracy or validity as the author has made no claims to be an expert and qualified on this topic. Notwithstanding, the reader is asked to do their own research and consult any subject matter experts they deem necessary to ensure the quality and accuracy of the material presented herein. By reading this document, the reader agrees that under no circumstances is the author responsible for any losses, direct or indirect, which are incurred because of the use of the information contained within this document, including, but not limited to, errors, omissions, or inaccuracies.

EXCLUSIVE BONUSES FOR YOUR SHADOW WORK JOURNEY

Welcome to the bonus page of my shadow work book! I have prepared ONE special gift for you that you can obtain by downloading the files through the QR code below.

BONUS #1: 5 DEEP EXERCISES TO EXPLORE YOUR SHADOW AND UNDERSTAND YOUR ARCHETYPES

This bonus that I offer is a series of guided and additional exercises to the books on shadow work. These exercises will help you deepen your work on the shadow and further develop your self-awareness.

I am excited to offer these bonuses to my readers and hope that they will help you further progress in your shadow work journey. Do not hesitate to download the files through the QR code below to access the bonuses and start exploring your shadow right away!

About this Shadow Workbook

Before reading this book, read this short section to know if this Shadow Workbook is for you or not. The purpose of this Workbook is to help you self-analyze so that you can eliminate your anxiety and negativity. To do this, the Shadow Workbook will follow a clear and concise path for your 21 Day journey. This 21 Day journey is your path to getting to know your inner child and your authentic self.

While you embark on your journey of self-actuation and get to know your inner child, there will be daily exercises for you to do. Each day you complete these exercises, you will check off a day on your Shadow Plan calendar. Every exercise that you do every day will help you explore your four main archetypes. These archetypes are the different parts of yourself that reside in your unconscious mind. Carl Jung said that it is the unconscious mind that dictates our daily life as well as the world around us.

As Carl Jung said, you need to keep in mind the world that is around you during your Shadow Plan journey. Your surroundings or environment can play a role in how you see yourself and, in turn, cause anxiety or negativity. While you're using this Shadow Workbook, you will be asked to observe your daily life and how you feel about the way people treat you. Along with this, it's important to evaluate the way that you treat yourself or look at yourself. It's important to follow the path of this workbook and stay dedicated to self-improvement for all 21 days.

TABLE OF CONTENTS

THE HOUSE OF THE COLLECTIVE UNCONSCIOUS

THE FLOORS of the house represent our consciousness, and the sun and light are our memories

We all breathe AIR to live and they are the values we share with others

THE FOUNDATIONS cannot be seen but hold up the structure of the whole house, they are our principles

THE GROUND is commonplace with all other people that Jung identifies as the collective unconscious

THE CELLAR of the house contains the things that we don't need or that we have forgotten, it carries our personal memories

THE WORKBOOK PATH

The path of this Workbook is specially designed to help you get to know your inner and authentic child and self through the exercises. These exercises are given to you as a tool to put the information that you'll learn to practical use and help you apply it. The information or content in this Workbook is Carl Jung's own works and his approach to psychology, explaining that our inner child dictates our own lives. He even devised methods to extract information about your inner child from your unconscious mind.

The content in this Workbook to help you extract this information is meditation techniques. The things that you would meditate on or contemplate are your four main archetypes and possible repressed ideas. You will learn about these repressed ideas and feelings while observing physical reactions to others or different thoughts. The exercises listed in this Workbook will help you learn about those repressed ideas and feelings.

Two exercises in this Workbook are a letter to your future self and a trigger log. The letter to your future self-extracts information about your desires and your hopes about where you wish to be. One of the reasons for this exercise is to also hope you imagine your life without anxiety and negativity. When you do, you'll begin to desire that life more and more, which invokes motivation for change. On the other hand, the trigger log exercise helps you identify the problems in your life. Sometimes we don't have the motivation to speak up when we feel wrong, and our body instinctually reacts. The build-up of these reactions to the negativity in our life causes anxiety and negativity. You will be expected to either make changes, so these reactions don't occur or instead complete a gratitude exercise to recharge your emotional batteries. It is the balance within yourself and acknowledging the authentic self that will give you relief from your anxiety or negativity.

To get to know your authentic self and create balance within yourself, it's important to get to know your four main archetypes. The content within this Workbook will go into great detail about this. You will also learn techniques to dive into your unconscious mind, which is what enables you to learn about your four main archetypes.

The exercises and techniques afforded to you in this Workbook will help you explore your desires and repressed feelings. You will take a trip through an exploration of your unconscious mind.

Exploring your unconscious mind may seem like a hard task, and you may get discouraged. If you do, remember that Carl Jung's methods of using the four main archetypes have helped many people live a better and more fulfilling life. If you have a broken bone or ear infection, you will go to a doctor, because they specialize in that area of expertise. In regard to how the mind works and the ways it can be modified, Carl Jung is a specialist in this area of expertise. It only makes sense that you would want advice from someone who has a vast knowledge of the topic that you are exploring.

You have made a good decision in choosing to learn about Carl Jung's four main archetypes. His methods will enable you to explore these four main archetypes in the comfort of your everyday life. With the methods listed in this Shadow Workbook, you will be able to begin your journey into your unconscious mind.

Why Use Carl Jung's Four Main Archetypes?

This journey into your unconscious mind will be into your Shadow, Persona, Anima, and Self. Exploring your desires, repressed ideas, and how the world sees you will afford you the knowledge of why you have anxiety and negativity. It's the exploration of these four main archetypes that will help you get to know your authentic self. We all have things about ourselves that we don't like, and during your journey, you will be able to get to the source of those things. Only through knowing yourself better can you begin to accept these characteristics about yourself. Once you accept them all, you can live a fuller life without anxiety and negativity.

If the source of your anxiety and negativity was in your everyday life and your conscious mind, you would need this Workbook. It will be with the use of Carl Jung's four main archetypes that you will be able to eliminate your anxiety and negativity. It's not uncommon for the four main archetypes to be affecting your daily life negatively enough. There is a lot in the world today to distract us and make it not a priority to change so that we are happier. Instant happiness can be found in watching our favorite shows and listening to the music that we like with a few easy taps on our phones. This instant happiness will last but a short time, which is why using this Shadow Workbook will help you in the long term.

You Could Use This Workbook If...

Social anxiety and negative thoughts about yourself can be helped by using Carl Jung's methods. If you feel like you're not living your full life, it's possibly because you have desires that are not being recognized and fulfilled. This book can be used to help you fulfill those very desires that are residing in your unconscious mind. You're reading this Workbook because you want to improve yourself and your life, so let's do it. Start using it and eliminate your anxiety and negativity.

If, after reading this, you choose to continue to read and use this book, it's time to start dedicating yourself to it. On the next page is this Workbook belongs-to declaration. You'll need to decide to dedicate yourself fully to this journey of getting to know yourself better. It's important to keep an open mind, so put your inhibitions aside and fill in that page.

THE BENEFITS OF SHADOW WORK

Transform your life

Overcome fears & traumas

Love yourself

Light up your shadow

Self-acceptance

Become 100% authentic

Deep self-awareness

This Shadow Workbook Belongs to:

Fill in with your name empty slots below and carefully read the following statements

I _____ pledge to read this Shadow Workbook from cover to cover, which I understand includes all the contents it holds. I agree to read every word and to use the information given for my self-reflection to achieve self-awareness. Using the contents of this Workbook, I fully intend to do my best to learn about my inner child with the intent to help me change any undesirable habits. I sign this with the full understanding that these exercises are intended to help me analyze both my subconscious and conscious so that I may perform these exercises to change unwanted habits.

I _____ pledge to perform all my daily exercises for the next 21 days consistently to ensure the most desirable outcome for myself. With this pledge, I know that the level of effort I put in is directly linked to the outcome and success of changing my habits. I also acknowledge that I dedicate to this Shadow Workbook and willingly undertake this endeavor with an open mind. I dedicate to exploring the authentic self within my subconscious and desire the healing of my inner child. I sign this with the intent to remove my anxiety and negativity to the best of my abilities and fully intend to complete this Shadow Workbook.

Date: _____

Sign Here: _____

"To confront a person with
his shadow is to show him
his own light."

- Carl Jung -

USING THIS WORKBOOK

When you begin using this Workbook, you may feel anxious about a lot of things. For example, you may feel anxious about being in a large group of people. In the beginning, before using this Workbook, you may even find it difficult to talk to people at work and make friends. While some days may seem hard, there is hope at the end of the tunnel awaiting you after your hard work. You can move past these feelings and eliminate your negativity and anxiety. If you begin using this Workbook to extinguish your negativity and or anxiety, you must be determined to see it through.

Do Nothing and Get Worse

By not working throw your anxiety and/or negativity, you will be allowing it to get worse. They will begin to bottle up like a shaken pop bottle. After a while, you will explode and no longer be able to function. It is essential that you take up your Workbook and begin your journey of self-improvement. You will begin your exploration of your inner child so that you can be your best self. By using this book with clear intentions and determination, you can get tangible, realistic results.

Workbook Results

If you want results and to improve yourself, then use this Workbook to the fullest. You don't have to be anxious when talking to coworkers. Being in a large group of people doesn't have to make you anxious but can bring you joy and make you happy. After using this book, you could dress the way you want and say what you want with full confidence in yourself. Say it loud and proud! You are strong, and you can do this.

PREFACE

Live not just to live, but to feel alive and self-aware. By asking yourself the question "why then dig deep into our inner child?", you can open a fascinating door. Why do some start the day off with a coffee and others with a cup of green tea? Could there be a reason why some get dressed first thing in the morning, as opposed to waiting till they walk out the door? The use of Shadow Workbook can be used by all as a tool to analyze their inner child by implementing Carl Jung's methods. These same methods can answer questions like "Why do I procrastinate?" and can also be applied to help remove anxiety and negativity just as effectively.

Hypothetically speaking, for example, you may be anxious about going about in public or entering a face-to-face social situation. It could be that you have very negative thoughts about your body or a particular physical characteristic. If either of these would apply to you, Carl Jung's methods and this Shadow Workbook could be just the tool you need to explore these real, understandable anxieties or negative thoughts. If so, then this book is for you, and the exercises in the daily explorations could very well help you.

One of the experiences that lie within this Shadow Workbook is a daily reminder to tell yourself that you are beautiful just the way you are and that whatever your particular characteristic or characteristics that you find undesirable are what make you unique. Your particular uniqueness is to be cherished and valued because it is priceless. This particular daily exercise is to tell yourself, "I love all my unique body characteristics, and I am worth being cherished because I am invaluable," in a mirror every morning while you brush your teeth or wash your face. You could use this exercise, and many more like it, to alleviate those anxious or negative thoughts that you are experiencing.

Carl Jung proposed with the Self archetype that anyone could see their self-worth and, with this knowledge, overcome any negative thoughts and/or anxiety.

The Persona archetype can help us understand why we feel like we aren't accepted by our peers. If our Persona archetype is in stark contrast or in conflict with our Self archetype, feelings of alienation can form in both our conscious and subconscious. It's possible for the characteristics that lie within our Shadow or Anima archetypes to be the source. It is these conflict warning within us that often cause anxiety and negativity. Carl Jung's methods within the exercises in this Shadow Workbook can help you explore this authentic self within your subconscious to ultimately relieve your anxieties and negativity.

INTRODUCTION

Have you ever thought that your behaviors are like those of your parents or grandparents? It is well established that children often walk or even talk the way their parents do. Carl Jung proposed that we inherit archetypes much like these inherited behaviors and proposed that there are four major archetypes. The four major archetypes are as listed: the Shadow, the Persona, the Anima / Animus, and the Self. Although, because they are inherited at such a young age, we must look to our subconscious or inner child to endeavor to root out the origin and its effect on our daily lives. This Shadow Workbook tries to explore the subconscious and bring these archetypes to the surface for analysis.

One of the archetypes that Jung proposed has been called the Shadow, which, as stated before, lies within the unconscious mind. It is made up of repressed ideas, wishes, impulses, and shortcomings. This Shadow contains the attributes of ourselves that we recognize are unacceptable to society and our own morals or beliefs. Carl Jung proposed that to fully know oneself, it is necessary to recognize and explore our Shadow archetype. This shadow can come forward and appear in dreams or visions in both a literal sense and through symbolism, and by analyzing this, one may attempt to analyze their shadow.

Another archetype this book endeavors to analyze is the Animus or Anima, which is the feminine appearance found within a male or the masculine appearance found within a female. Carl Jung postulated that these appearances contribute to our gender identity and even sexual roles. Considering society's rigid gender roles, an Anima would pose defiance to social norms and would be pushed to the subconscious. By looking in the mirror and participating in this Shadow Workbook exercises, it becomes possible to analyze this particular archetype, as well as the others, using the exercises in this Shadow Workbook.

Looking in the mirror, the Persona archetype can also begin to surface through the exercises in the Shadow Workbook. One's Persona is a mask or change in behavior that can be contributed to a certain social setting or persons in attendance. Carl Jung postulates that this persona or mask develops to shield us and suppress our urges. In direct correlation with emotional outbursts, not being socially acceptable in a public environment will create a persona to suppress the impulse. While one's Persona could arguably be a characteristic of oneself, Carl Jung would say that the Self is another thing altogether.

The archetype of the Self is comprised of both the unconscious and subconscious within a person. Within your unconscious and subconscious, there are personality traits that exist, which in turn are the Self. Every attribute and characteristic that lie within and make up someone's personality, knowing or unknowing, can be attributed to the Self archetype. As Carl Jung often explained, it is like a circle with a dot in the center, representing one's ego, and the circle being the Self. The relationship between your ego and the Self archetype is what gives it its importance. The Shadow Workbook daily entries will guide you on a path and help you analyze each one of these archetypes within yourself. Through self-awareness and understanding comes growth and personal knowledge. After finishing and participating in each daily exercise, it is hoped that you can find a deeper understanding of your inner child. While your inner child or unconscious is not obviously there, it is undoubtedly prevalent in your daily life. The unconscious mind is a powerful force with our personality / inner child that ultimately dictates our actions or reactions.

Carl Jung would say that the unconscious mind rules our lives and that only by understanding our unconscious mind and inner child we truly take hold of our lives. Take back your power, explore your unconscious mind, and get to know your inner child. It will no longer rule your day and cause you anxiety or negativity because you're taking back the power. Ultimately, this is how you can self-improve and get rid of your anxiety and negativity. During the 21 days, it will be a conscious decision to self-improve every day, but after, it will be a habit and become a part of your authentic self, which will allow you to do it almost effortlessly.

You may still get anxious thoughts, but a rush of endorphins and positive thoughts will allow you to move on. With the completion of the Shadow Workbook comes clear a journey of self-improvement and a feeling of improved self-esteem. You can do this!

"Shadow work is the path
of the heart warrior".

- G.C. Jung -

INTRODUCTION TO
CARL JUNG

Carl Jung was born on July 26th, 1875, and he was the founder of analytic psychology. His analytic psychology also included the study of the collective unconscious. He also studied the real correlation between illogical responses to stimulus words. He was able to find out that most mental illnesses were caused by emotionally charged clusters that could be attributed to unconsciousness. His finds were solidified by Freud's ideas, as they were contingent on one another on this account. Carl Jung's methods look to our shadows; he suggested that we have hidden anxieties and repressed thoughts. His methods of analysis strive to pull out the unconscious into the conscious in an attempt for self-improvement and being self-aware.

To the Shadow Workbook Content

This Shadow Workbook content endeavors to help reshape the readers' habits within 21 days to eliminate negativity and anxiety. "Why 21 days?", you may ask. According to Maxwell Maltz, it takes 21 days to change a habit: therefore, it's a 21-day challenge. The Shadow Workbook will talk about those possible habits that you want to change during your 21-day journey.

WHAT IS SHADOW WORK?

A few habits that you might want to change are, as mentioned: going to bed late, doing work while you eat, not taking time to relax each day, or even leaving stuff laying around instead of putting it away immediately. The daily reflection exercises can help you find the reason why you hold on to these bad habits and find it difficult to change them. Many people find it very hard to spend less time on social media and instead spend more time on themselves or in direct contact with people. Plus, with increased social media presence, it can occur almost an obsession with one's physical appearance and perceived shortcomings. Carl Jung suggested that it is necessary to know that all aspects of yourself, both subconscious and conscious, are fulfilled. In fact, Carl Jung believed that you could not change anything unless you first accepted it. By understanding the four main archetypes and following this 21-day plan, you too can change those bad habits and become self-aware.

Analyzing the Self archetype and all its parts daily is just one way you can become more self-aware. When you're talking to a coworker or friend, and they say something that evokes a feeling in you, stop and ask yourself why. If you have negative thoughts like "I can't do that," ask yourself, "Why can't I do that?" Maybe the reason you can't go to bed early enough is that you believe you haven't done enough or your desired achievements of the day were not reached. Go easy on yourself and look closely at what your hopes, desires, and beliefs are. Your personality is made up of those hopes and desires, but another aspect is your ego and unconscious mind. The ego has a few components, like the focus on survival, pleasure, perception of others, and desire for success or achievement. Your unconscious mind is composed of the unknown aspects of your personality. By identifying your conscious attributes, like your point of view, beliefs, feelings, and thoughts, you can explore the unconscious. With this Shadow Workbook 21-day plan, you can use the Self archetype to unearth why it's so difficult to put work aside and just eat your meal.

Unlike the inability to put work aside to eat, the compulsion to constantly be on social media can stem from an Anima or Animus. If there is an anomaly that others or you see as particular, personality may compel us to seek validation. While it more commonly presents itself in adolescents, a feminine or masculine physical characteristic that society or you have deemed to be an abnormality can compel us to get likes online. One look in a mirror may say there's a particular feature that is found unbecoming, and if that feature is excited on or constantly reminded of it, that becomes an Anima. Oftentimes, the Anima is created because of social norms or outside forces, and through self-assurance and daily reminders, this Anima will no longer be the driving force in our lives.

Carl Jung hit it right on the mark when he said, "the most terrifying thing is to accept oneself completely." It is also true that there is a sense of relief and confidence afterward. If your Anima resides more in your unconscious thoughts, it may result in repressed ideas. Those repressed thoughts or ideas are an aspect or component of your Shadow.

The Shadow is made up of a lot of attributes or components like weaknesses, desires, instincts, and maybe even perceived shortcomings. If your instincts tell you to just go and go without stopping, you could find yourself constantly taking things out and not putting them back. This behavior can stem from anxiety and feelings of shortcomings like you're not doing enough in the day or a subconscious deep desire to do more. One exercise you could do is taking a deep breath after finishing a task to slow down and then say to yourself, "I did a good job." The act of slowing down and taking one task at a time can help lower your anxiety while saying to yourself, "I did a good job" will help alleviate any anxiety about how the task was completed. The Workbook content aims to follow and look at each one of the four archetypes and analyze your reactions accordingly. This process will help find the target source and it will lead you to a solution.

What Are the Four Archetypes?

The four main archetypes are as listed: the Self, the Anima, the Persona, and the Shadow. Each of these four archetypes provides a specific exploration into your subconscious and authentic self. It is possible for them to appear overlapped, but this is only because your authentic self is deeply intertwined in each one of these four archetypes. As an example, one might alter their behavior because of the Anima and, in turn, modify their Persona accordingly. Following the modification, a distinct contrast between the Self and the Persona may occur, which causes anxiety and negativity. It's through the exploration of the Shadow that anyone can be allowed to identify these conflicts and imbalances within our authentic selves. That being said, let's begin the exploration of each one of these four archetypes so that you may better understand them and embark on your journey.

The Self archetype is an archetype that has fewer components and yet is the cornerstone to exploring the causes of someone's anxiety and negativity. The three components to exploring the self are your personality type, the ego, and the unconscious. The Self is created through the process that is known as individuation. Think of individuation as the various characteristics of the personality integrated into a separate thing when the personality and ego interact. Jung believed the imbalance between the subconscious and conscious is the cause of anxiety and negativity, which means the four archetypes must work in tangent with one another. To understand the Self, let's begin defining the ego and the personality.

The ego is a person's self-esteem and self-worth, while the personality is the characteristics or qualities that make up a person's character. That being said, you may be wondering how your character is affected by your self-esteem or self-worth. Knowing how one affects the other will allow you to analyze the creation of the Self, and through this exploration, you will be able to know your authentic self.

Another archetype in your authentic self is the Anima, and while it commonly resides in the conscience, when there is a conflict with the Self archetype, it can be pushed to the subconscious. When this happens, exploration becomes a necessity because of how the formation of anxiety and negativity can be created. The Anima corresponds to feminine attributes or characteristics, both physical and mental, that appear in a male. Whereas the Anima that appears within females corresponds to attributes or characteristics, both physical and mental, that are typically masculine. With a simple look in a full-body mirror, physical attributes or characteristics can be identified, which in term allow us to identify an obvious Anima. On the other hand, mental/psychological attributes or characteristics require self-reflection. If these mental/psychological attributes or characteristics have been pushed to the subconscious, the self-reflection may require lots of thinking and may result in some painful realizations. Carl Jung once said, though, "There's no coming to conscious without pain." In many cases, pain can be a good thing when used to motivate us to make progress. Our body's natural response to pain, however, tends to be to turn away from it because of societal norms that suppose that pain is a bad thing. The Persona archetype is created to protect us from it; knowing this, we can begin exploring it.

The Persona archetype is the person or persona we project outwardly to others or even characteristics and attributes we have that can be directly linked to society. When applying the Persona archetype to the endeavor of exploring our anxieties and negativity, it's helpful to observe our behavioral changes, even thoughts or feelings. When you are alone, does your behavior differ from when you are with family or friends? When answering this question, don't think about activities that you would participate in, but about mannerisms or how you carry yourself. When you're alone, do you slouch? When you're with your friends and family, do you sit up perfectly straight? If this applies to you, it's very possible that you become anxious about how you hold your body.

Say, for instance, that when you're around your family, they constantly correct your grammar; this could result in negative thoughts towards yourself like you're not smart enough. While this may not be true or even conscious, your subconscious mind could interpret those words as such. In this example, it would be to your benefit to remind yourself that you are smart and that you do have worth. Some may take the approach of just widening their vocabulary and brushing up on their English language skills. Either of these approaches is healthy and could result in the alleviation of anxiety and/or negativity. Keep in mind that the Shadow archetype plays a fundamental role in the creation of the Persona.

"How much do I keep in mind, though?", you may ask yourself. Well, the Shadow is composed of the following: repressed ideas or feelings, perceived weaknesses, desires, instincts, and shortcomings. When these aspects of the Shadow interact with the other archetypes, additional attributes or characteristics of the Shadow can form. These are envy, greed, prejudice, hate, and even aggression. When these additional characteristics or attributes form, they result in anxiety and negativity, which, if you wish to eliminate them, must be explored. For Carl Jung said, "We cannot change anything unless we accept it." As you may very well know, a crucial part of accepting something is that you know what that something is.

This Shadow Workbook will help you tap into your unconscious mind and show you just how powerful it is. You will learn about your triggers and why they occur. While using this Workbook, you will gain knowledge of the source of your anxiety and negativity. Your unconscious and inner child know the true source, and through the exploration of your authentic self, so will you. It will take a 21-day commitment, which is okay because you can do it!

Now you can do an exercise to explore these four main archetypes. To explore your Self archetype, reflect on your basic desires and what your body or mind instinctively wants. For this experience, ask yourself, "What can I do to feel more like myself and booster my self-esteem?" When exploring the Anima archetype, try looking at yourself in the mirror. As you may have seen on TV, bullies will shame people for being different. It's possible that you are doing this to yourself. The next step to this experience is to list five attributes, either physical or mental, that you like about yourself. Listing five ways you are different when you're not alone is a good way to explore the Persona archetype. Finally, it's time to explore your Shadow archetype by listing five perceived weaknesses or shortcomings.

Desires

1) _____

2) _____

3) _____

4) _____

5) _____

Self-esteem boosters

1) _____

2) _____

3) _____

4) _____

5) _____

Good attributes

1) _____

2) _____

3) _____

4) _____

5) _____

Ways I change

1) _____

2) _____

3) _____

4) _____

5) _____

Weaknesses or shortcomings

1) _____

2) _____

3) _____

4) _____

5) _____

After completing the exercise, you may begin to wonder what that accomplished or how that could help you. Fulfilling your desires is the path to feeling happier and feeling like you are getting the most out of life. If you are, you can be confident about your choices and not feel anxious about them or even negative. The choice to love yourself the way you are helps eliminate negative feelings towards yourself about how you look or act. When you list your good attributes, you also boost your self-esteem because you're focusing on the good things and not just on the bad ones. Too often, you focus on those because we are wired to do so to help us survive. Focusing on the bad things too much negatively impacts our lives, so it's important to adapt and change those tendencies to survive. That's why listing five ways you can change for the better is so beneficial. If there were no changes that you needed to make in your life, you wouldn't be feeling anxious or negative. One way to find possible changes that need to happen is by acknowledging your shortcomings and weaknesses. It's during these 21 days of exercises that you will be able to explore these lists more to eliminate your anxiety and negativity.

What Does the Shadow Workbook Accomplish?

During the 21 days of exercises within this Shadow Workbook, you will identify your triggers and accomplish the elimination of your anxiety and negativity. You'll be able to eliminate them by finding the sources of those triggers. After finding the sources, you can begin the process of making changes within your life that will ultimately eliminate your negativity and anxiety. It is also quite possible that by getting to know your authentic self/shadow self, your anxieties and negativities will be eliminated. For some, strictly the understanding of "why" can do wonders.

MEETING YOUR SHADOW SELF!

The wonderful knowledge and the carefully constructed 21 days of exercises that lie within this Workbook are amazing. You will be able to really get to know your authentic/shadow self and, by doing so, eliminate your negativity and anxiety. The carefully constructed exercises will explore the four main archetypes that make up your shadow self. With these archetypes, your exploration will take a clear path. You will get to know your Shadow, Anima, Persona, and Self archetypes of yourself.

Why Analyze Your Shadow Self?

You may be saying, "why can't you just tell me what I am supposed to be doing? I'll do it." The answer to that is really not that simple because everyone has their unique analysis; humans are very complex. It's only through analyzing yourself and doing the daily exercises that you can begin to make the necessary changes. These are paramount for the elimination of your anxiety and negativity. At times, it may seem like only the bad things are surfacing, but remember that where it is bad, there is an equal amount of good. Good lies within everyone, and yes, that means you too. Maybe you're messing up a lot at work or with friends and you think that makes you a bad person. You can be wrong. Everyone messes up and needs to adjust how they are doing something if it's not working. All that is required to be a good person is to keep trying and remind us that we all make mistakes. Good lies within us all. If you feel like there isn't enough good residing. within yourself, this Workbook can help you find it. Reading it does more than just analyze mistakes and negative feelings. While on your journey, you will be exploring your inner child and getting to know your authentic self. Carl Jung believed no one is inherently good or bad, but it is our actions and the choices we make that make us so. You are endeavoring to improve yourself, and that choice reflects who you are as a person.

What Good Lies Within?

Carl Jung also said that getting to know your shadow self can not only help you understand the bad things that you are capable of, but also the good ones. To get to know the good that lies within, you must get to the root of your desires, hopes, and dreams. It is the unconscious mind, your authentic self, that is the driving force for your daily habits or even your desires. It really will help to discover your personal unconscious and to learn what makes you tick or what motivates you.

Knowing that good lies within you will also help you stay positive. Too often, we give up because we think it's hopeless, but the Shadow Workbook can show you that, actually, it's not hopeless at all. You can find the good that lies within you. When you see someone hurting, I'm sure you empathize with them, and it hurts you that they are in pain. It's indeed hard to find the good in yourself and have good self-esteem when you're getting anxious and negative all day, every day. That's why it's so important that you embark on your self-improvement journey to get to know your inner child.

Self-Esteem

It's very hard not to be anxious or negative when you don't appreciate your full self. With thoughts like, "I can never be a good spouse or parent," or even, "I'm too stupid to do anything right," you won't be able to eliminate your anxiety. It is crucial to love yourself, for only through caring and effort can change come about. You are worth caring about! The fact that you are reading this is evidence enough that you care about yourself and want to self-improve.

Will My Life Be Better for It?

Your life can get better by using this book, and in many different ways too. For starters, your relationships will improve because you'll have more mental energy to have fun.

Without that emotional anvil on your chest, you will have inner peace present in every second of the day. You'll be able to go out for a walk and fully take in every moment of the birds chirping or the wind on your face. Listening to your loved ones talk about their day will be fun and could be the highlight of your day again.

Can Using the Shadow Workbook Be Hard?

It is true: getting to a good point again won't be easy, but nothing worth obtaining is. Any time you self-reflect and look inwards, you could find something hard to deal with. It may take some time to look inside yourself, and with the world we live in, that can be hard. You know it's important to eliminate your anxiety and negativity. Inevitably, a change of any kind can be and is indubitably difficult, but it is worth it. And so it can be using The Shadow Workbook to eliminate your anxiety and negativity. While using this Workbook, you will be diving into repressed ideas and memories, so you'll need to deal with those feelings when they come to the surface. They were repressed because, at the time, your mind thought you couldn't process them, but they are still affecting you. It's imperative to remember you are stronger now. The hardness of those feelings will be replaced with life without anxiety and negativity once you process them. You can be happier by working through this hardship in the foreseeable future. The journey that you will embark on with this book is worth it.

The Exploration

In this book, you will go on an exploration of your psyche to discover the solution to eliminating your anxiety and negativity. While diving into your four archetypes, the Self, the Anima, the Shadow, and the Persona, you will find long-lost information about your inner child. With this knowledge, you will get to know your authentic self and find what can bring you joy within the hardship. You'll be able to answer questions like, "Why do I get so anxious when strangers talk to me at the store?"

While you will not have control over what you learn about yourself, it is crucial to do so. Although, after discovering what's within your unconscious, giving you a better understanding of yourself is important to continue your journey. It's not only important but necessary, as you are in an ongoing process of self-improvement. Don't expect perfection at any point in your journey because it is an unattainable goal, as perfection is subjective. You are on an ongoing journey on a path to self-improvement!

While you self-improve, it will be necessary for you to self-analyze. Self-analyzing is a key point in Carl Jung's method. He said, "knowing your own darkness is the best method for dealing with the darkness of other people." It's the confidence and self-assurance within ourselves that allows us to have the strength to deal with everyday life.

While it's true the journey to self-improvement is not easy, because getting to know yourself may be painful, he also said, "There's no coming to consciousness without pain." He knew that things reside within our unconscious minds for a reason, and while the healing process is needed to bring it to the conscious, it is painful. Your mind can never repress anything fully, so though you may not be aware of the source of your anxiety and negativity, your brain does know. The good news is you don't have to be what happens to you, but what you choose to become; Carl Jung also believed this.

During your exploration, you will be endeavoring to pull your unconscious mind into your conscious mind. To bring your unconscious mind forward, you will need to look deeper into your own self and soul. Carl Jung said: "your visions will become clear only when you look into yourself and self-reflect on any possible meanings". It is now your goal to do just that and look into your heart. Go forward and self-analyze every aspect of your life, both small and big. He believed that there were no irrelevant aspects of our lives. Begin your journey by observing your life and self-analyzing.

The Analysis of Myself

While on this journey to self-improvement, you will be expected to analyze yourself. While using the Workbook to analyze yourself and by using the exercises, you will be able to identify target problems, which will give you the ability to postulate a solution. Below are possible problems that may be found after exploring your authentic self with this Workbook and could be the source of anxiety or negativity. Also listed below are possible solutions for things that can be changed to help eliminate problems and the corresponding anxiety or negativity.

How Do You Do Self Analysis?

The first thing you'll do is to identify a problem that's consciously causing you anxiety or negativity. Next, really think about your authentic self and how the four archetypes could be the unconscious source. Finally, you will be capable of devising a solution, which could consist of a change in perspective or a behavior change. Now that you are aware of all the steps, you may be wondering, "Well, how do I identify the problem or conscious cause of my anxiety and negativity?"

You identify a problem by listening to your body and observing its reactions to your surroundings. Some possible reactions are tightness of the chest or hypervigilance; both are evidence that you're feeling anxious or negative. An example of a surrounding you may be in is a crowded room or alone in your home. It's only after you identify that there is a problem that you can meditate on what it could be about. Thoughts will cross your mind, and once you have identified what the problem is, your symptoms will subside a little. Your brain knows that identifying the problem is the first step to eliminating the issue.

Now that you have found out what the problem is, you can use the four archetypes to determine what the cause actually is. As stated before, the four archetypes are the Shadow, the Self, the Anima, and the Persona.

If the problem is you get anxious when you're at home alone and feel negative about yourself, we can begin to postulate. The Shadow archetype could quite possibly desire lots of human interaction or large amounts of stimuli. The Self might believe that not having people around you or people to talk to must mean you are undesirable. The Anima may think that society says we need to be around people, and not being around people means there's something wrong. While, on the other hand, the Persona could be out of balance because you give an outward appearance of being a people person. People persons have people to hang out with, and if you do not, that disrupts the Persona you have displayed.

If these archetypes conflict with one another and they are not all working in tangent, the solution is obvious. It is paramount that you begin to hang out and talk to people regularly. Don't think about it as if your mental health relies solely on others, but that you like being around people and can't deny that part of yourself. On the other hand, if you find that your four archetypes were against each other, that is evidence of a deeper personal imbalance. If this is happening, then it's possible you are denying who you are as a person. Just because society says you should want to be around people doesn't mean you necessarily have to. The same can be said if a part of you wants to be around people, but another part says that you'll get hurt, so you shouldn't want to. Life is not worth living without there being some risk, and it's okay to get sometimes hurt as long as we pick ourselves back up again. Here are some other possible problems and solutions following the Carl Jung method.

POSSIBLE PROBLEMS AND SOLUTIONS

Problem #1
Being in Public Makes Me Anxious

Possible Authentic Self Realizations

- **The Shadow:** Within my subconscious resides the idea that I must stay home, for home is my safe place. My desires and wants have put my home as a good place more than anywhere else. Given the fact that I have been hurt while not at home, I desire to stay away from that potential pain.

- **The Self:** My ego/self-esteem was damaged when I was in public due to bullying and the inability to have the same mannerisms as others. My personality dictates that I hold my head high and defend others in their time of need. How am I supposed to hold my head high or defend others when I feel unable to do so?

- **The Anima:** My mannerisms are more masculine, and others find them to be confrontational. Being that I am not a confrontational person and my personality is quite warm and loving of others, I am facing a conflict within myself.

- **The Persona:** Due to repressed trauma out in public, my Persona in public is confrontational and adversarial. My authentic self has changed my Persona in this way as a coping mechanism to protect myself.

Changes I Can Make

I must confront my trauma and remind myself that it's okay to grieve so that I may alleviate my anxiety and/or negativity. Carl Jung said, "I am not what happened to me; I am what I choose to become." With this fact, I can also remind myself that lightning never strikes twice in the same place. By processing my trauma, my mannerisms may in fact, change. If they do not, that would be fine too because I can remember that my authentic self is one that protects me. Inside my ego is a person that knows I'm worth protecting; therefore, I should be proud of my mannerisms. As for my Persona, a mere explanation to those around me that I care about could alleviate any conflicts. With the absence of conflicts with others, I could alleviate the conflict within myself, and in turn, alleviate my anxiety and negativity.

Problem #2
I Don't Like the Way I Look

Possible Authentic Self Realizations

- **The Shadow:** I desire to shine, and while it may be an immature desire, it is a part of who I am. It's important not to repress this desire and to live life to my fullest, so I will accept this desire as a part of my authentic self. One of my shortcomings is that I often put others' desires before my own.

- **The Self:** My ego suffers when I let others' desires before my own. My personality dictates that I persevere and follow my instincts to live for who I am without reprieve. To live for myself and follow my desires unapologetically is my authentic self, and I acknowledge that only by doing so can I eliminate my anxieties and negativity. My Self does not allow others to dictate who I am.

- **The Anima:** I prefer short hair, but short hair is for boys.

- **The Persona:** I think things as efficiently as possible, and I feel like having long hair isn't efficient because it takes more maintenance.

Changes I Can Make

The first thing I can change is to wear the shining jewelry and accessories that I like proudly. I will remind myself that these are the things that my authentic self likes, and to live for myself to the fullest I must let my Self be happy with them. The next thing I will do is cut my hair short and let everyone close to me know that I love my hair and it expresses who I am on the inside. I will remind myself that if people really cared about me, they wouldn't want me to be anxious or not about how I look. In addition, I would tell myself this is who I am, and it's a good thing to show it to the world.

Problem #3
When People Come Over to My House, I Have Anxiety and Worry About What They'll Think

Possible Authentic Self Realizations

- **The Shadow:** I desire others' approval to reinforce that I am doing a good job. One of my repressed ideas is that because of my upbringing, I don't have the necessary skills to make a good home. While I have the desire, like many others, to do so because of my instinct to have a warm and inviting home, I often doubt myself. It's fair to say that I even envy others that were brought up in a way that taught them how to make a warm and inviting home.

- **The Self:** My self-esteem is hinged on others' approval of my actions and accomplishments. This can be directly linked to my personality's tendency to need others around because I am an extrovert.

- **The Anima:** I find inter design difficult, and often my sense of taste does not align with social norms. A typical female characteristic is the ability to belong and interact within a village of people. My Anima is such that I gravitate more towards groups of three or four because I desire a more personal interaction. My anxieties and negativity come to a head when I have gatherings because, more often than not, they are all larger than I desire. I do this because I think it matters that everyone can find their small three or four people they can interact with.

- **The Persona:** Sometimes, I project the person I believe I'm supposed to be and not the person I am to gain acceptance or approval from those I care about. My Persona represents me as a well-adjusted female that is also an experienced hostess.

Changes I Can Make

With the realizations that I have made and in the name of being my authentic self, I would first remind myself that if I'm not happy, no one can be happy when they come over. People know when you are anxious or stressed, and they tend to feel those same feelings too, out of empathy. Next, I would remind myself that it's my home, and If I'm happy with It, others that truly care about me will also be happy with it. My Anima makes me special, and so my next step would be reminding myself I am cherished and loved for who I am, not for what I do. When people come over to my home, I will choose to see me and not my stuff. Finally, I could become more well-adjusted and learn more about hosting by observing others. It's also within my power to read up on the topic beforehand and ask others for feedback the next time.

NOW YOU!

Problem:

_____

Possible Authentic Self-Realizations:

The Shadow _____

_____

_____

_____

_____

The Self _____

_____

_____

_____

_____

The Anima _____

_____

_____

_____

_____

The Persona _____

_____

_____

_____

_____

Solution:

_____

_____

_____

_____

_____

_____

_____

_____

_____

_____

_____

_____

_____

_____

_____

_____

Problem:

_____

Possible Authentic Self-Realizations:

The Shadow _____

_____

_____

_____

_____

The Self _____

_____

_____

_____

_____

The Anima _____

_____

_____

_____

_____

The Persona _____

_____

_____

_____

_____

Solution:

_____

_____

_____

_____

_____

_____

_____

_____

_____

_____

_____

_____

_____

_____

_____

_____

_____

_____

_____

Problem:

_____

Possible Authentic Self-Realizations:

The Shadow _____

_____

_____

_____

_____

The Self _____

_____

_____

_____

_____

The Anima _____

_____

_____

_____

_____

The Persona _____

_____

_____

_____

_____

_____

Solution:

_____

_____

_____

_____

_____

_____

_____

_____

_____

_____

_____

_____

_____

_____

_____

_____

_____

_____

Exercise Explanation

Doing this exercise will help you find the source of the problem. You are endeavoring to learn more about your inner child, comprised of these four main archetypes. While you keep that problem in mind, keep these four main archetypes in mind too, to analyze yourself healthily. It's only so that your analysis of self-improvement can occur.

Why? How Will This Help Me?

If you understand the source of your problem, you can work to eliminate your anxiety and negativity. Doing so will enable you to find some inner peace. Going through each day with a weight on your chest is exhausting. Your days will be much more enjoyable if you're not weighed down by your anxiety and negativity.

MUST DO'S!

Keeping an open mind is key for all these exercises and for any progress to be made. If you think there's no more you can learn about yourself, then there won't be anything more you will learn about yourself. You know that there's a problem and that improvement needs to be made, or you wouldn't be reading this book. Now you have to say to yourself that it's okay and that we're all on our own journey. Next, have clean intentions while reading every word and doing your Shadow Plan. The more goal-oriented you are, the higher the probability that you will achieve your goal. To do so, you must also be consistent because this allows behavioral changes. If your brain has an oath not to change, it most definitely will not, because who likes to change? Changes are uncomfortable. To eliminate your negativity and anxiety, you must be determined and unwavering. So, let's begin your journey of self-improvement and identify those triggers.

What Are Triggers?

When we think about triggers, we think about emotional responses, and that would be correct. A trigger is a cause of an event or situation you are in. Given that the issue at hand is anxiety and negativity, we can conclude that the event or situation you are in is being anxious and/or negative. These feelings alert you through a trigger, and only through observing your environment can you know what that trigger is. A possible trigger could be being in a loud, crowded room or people watching you eat. The thing triggering you could be either conscious or unconscious. The point of this Shadow Workbook and constructing a Shadow Plan is to identify the triggers.

Possible Triggers

A possible trigger that you could identify is having anxiety about being alone at home and not talking to anyone. It could be that you don't have object permanence and that not having someone right there gives you the feeling that you have no one. Another possibility is that you're triggered by people watching you eat. One of the reasons why this might trigger you is because you are self-conscious about how you look. Making a purchase, even for something that's a necessity, could make you anxious and be a trigger. If you grew up not having enough or feel like those around you make much more than you do, this could be the cause of your trigger. Once you identify your triggers, healing can begin.

To begin the journey of removing your anxieties and negativity, the first step is to identify triggers to analyze your authentic self within your subconscious. Once we know the triggers, we can begin the process of analyzing them to find their root and ultimately alleviate anxiety or negativity. For your first full day using this Shadow Workbook, pay attention to how things make you feel. Whenever you feel anxious, take up your Workbook and document the event for later reflection. If there aren't enough spots, that's okay because you can use a blank sheet of paper and answer the same questions listed below. Let's begin the first step...

EXERCISE: TRIGGER LOG

Trigger Alert!!!

What Triggered You:

_____

_____

_____

_____

Who Triggered You:

_____

_____

_____

_____

How Did You Feel:

_____

_____

_____

_____

When Did It Happen:

_____

_____

_____

_____

Where Were You:

_____

_____

_____

_____

Extra Notes:

_____

_____

_____

_____

_____

_____

_____

_____

_____

_____

_____

_____

_____

_____

_____

_____

_____

_____

Trigger Alert!!!

What Triggered You:

_____

_____

_____

_____

Who Triggered You:

_____

_____

_____

_____

How Did You Feel:

_____

_____

_____

_____

When Did It Happen:

_____

_____

_____

_____

Where Were You:

_____

_____

_____

_____

Extra Notes:

_____

_____

_____

_____

_____

_____

_____

_____

_____

_____

_____

_____

_____

_____

_____

_____

Trigger Alert!!!

What Triggered You:

_____
_____
_____
_____

Who Triggered You:

_____
_____
_____
_____

How Did You Feel:

_____
_____
_____
_____

When Did It Happen:

_____
_____
_____
_____

Where Were You:

_____

_____

_____

_____

Extra Notes:

_____

_____

_____

_____

_____

_____

_____

_____

_____

_____

_____

_____

_____

_____

_____

_____

_____

TRIGGER REFLECTION

Think about your triggers impact your daily behaviors. Are there things you avoid or don't like to do because you're afraid they might trigger you? How do you try to recover after you've been triggered?

_____

_____

_____

_____

_____

_____

_____

_____

_____

_____

_____

_____

_____

_____

_____

_____

_____

_____

_____

_____

Exercise Explanation

Completing this exercise will enable you to be more aware of the specific things that trigger you. A person that used to be famous once said, "Knowing is half the battle." That's why answering what, when, where, and how can allow you to analyze the trigger. The extra notes section is for your thoughts and self-reflection on the trigger in question. Your trigger may not be obvious at first because of the overwhelming feelings that may be clouding it.

It's possible that talking to people makes you anxious because you're worried about how they will react to what you said. It is equally possible that you look up to someone and you're afraid of messing up in front of them. Even having negative thoughts about your choice at lunch could stem from a past of bad eating habits. That is why you must answer all the questions with great thought and effort.

Why? How Will This Help?

"Why must I put great thought and effort into answering these questions?" you may ask. The answer to that is quite simple. Only through deep contemplation can you truly find what's actually triggering you. Sometimes, our triggers like to play peekaboo and only briefly reveal themselves to us. By answering these questions and participating fully in the exercise, you will be able to identify your trigger honestly.

Analyzing Your Triggers

Looking back on your day, how did these triggers affect your behavior throughout the day? First, organize your triggers from "it completely changed my day" to "I barely remembered what happened." Can the ones that affected you the most be avoided? Could telling someone about the trigger alleviate it? If there are triggers that you barely remember, why did they affect you so much at the time? What did or could you do to turn your day back around after you have been triggered?

Write down all the answers to these questions below along with why you think you are triggered.

_____

_____

_____

_____

_____

_____

_____

_____

_____

_____

_____

_____

Now that you have completed today's exploration of yourself, try and do some self-care or do some extra things that are right for you. After an emotional endeavor, it's important to recharge your emotional batteries. After completing an exercise like the trigger log, try doing something like taking a bubble bath or going for a walk in the woods. Do just about anything that brings you joy and recharges your emotional batteries. Keeping them as full as possible will make the process of eliminating your anxiety and negativity significantly easier.

OUR REALITY

Carl Jung said our inner child is formed through the interaction of the world around us and those in it. Your reality is not only the people that are closest to you but also the things they say to you and what you perceive them to have done to you. While we create our reality at the basic level with our five senses, there is a whole other level to reality.

This other level of our reality is created within our mind and is done through what we perceive others to have done. We use a method called cause and effect to establish the attributes of all four of our archetypes. For example, if someone with a space in between their two top buck teeth made a high-pitched sound every time they talked, and other people laughed, that would be the cause. The inevitable effect would be that they felt uncomfortable being laughed at and would hate their teeth. What you do at that moment will cement what type of person you are. At this moment, you want to eliminate your negativity and anxiety. You know the effect it's having on your life right now, but the question is what in your reality is causing it. One way to alleviate the causes of your anxiety and negativity is to find out what affects them. You have learned about triggers, so let's explore your reality to understand your conscience and subconscious self better.

An Exploration Into Your Self

It's another day, and you have officially committed to completing all 21 days of self-exploration into your authentic self. Now that you have identified some triggers, the next thing to do is to get to know your shadow self. To get to know it, and ultimately your authentic self, it's important to put everything on the table. Jung believed that all people are made up of three different parts, which are the ego, the personal unconscious, and the collective unconscious.

The Ego

The ego is quite simply your conscious self and what you can consider to be you. When someone says that a person has a big ego, they are saying that person is full of themselves. If you wake up every morning and do your self-care, a part of your ego cares about your appearance. Exploring the four major archetypes can help you understand why that exactly is. Another possible characteristic of your ego could be that you are eco-conscious. If you are very eco-conscious, then you might wear hemp clothes or might use animal cruelty-free products. Both examples are possible characteristics of your ego.

The Personal Unconscious

On the other hand, the personal unconscious is the repressed ideas or memories that lie within the mind. They have been put off to the side, and they are an instrumental aspect of who you are. The memories or ideas that lie within your personal unconscious must be accessed to make any self-improvement. An example of personal traumatic memories that may have been repressed from your childhood would be if you were attacked by a dog. Well, it's possible you don't remember being attacked by a dog, but it happened; therefore, it affects you. These repressed ideas or memories are just one reason why sharing this Workbook with others in your life may be helpful. You could meditate to bring these memories to the surface, or you could also talk to those around you who would remember and know them.

The Collective Unconscious

The collective unconscious won't be so easy to access. These are repressed impulses or beliefs. Some examples of your collective unconscious in your daily life may be the feeling of déjà vu or even love at first sight. Even something such as being afraid of monsters can be a part of it because of society. The collective unconscious mind is rooted in the idea that our culture inevitably shapes who we are as a person. One exercise you can do to fully explore your reality is to write on the line the first thing that comes to mind.

EXERCISE: WHO AM I?

My name is _____. I am _____ years old, and I spend my spare time _____. I also love to _____, _____, _____, and _____.

These are just a few things that allow my authentic self to shine and give me happiness. I am a good person and I know myself better than anyone.

Three words that I would use to describe myself are _____, _____, and _____. I am a good _____ and I'm great at _____. I love that I can _____, _____, and _____ well. Someday I want to_____.

One of my dreams is to _____ _____. I would like to go on a trip with _____. Some other important people to me are _____, _____, and _____.

Three things that I have done that I'm proud of are _____, _____, and _____. After doing those things I felt _____ and _____. I can feel that same way after completing daily essential tasks like _____, _____, and _____. If the tiniest of mistakes matter, then so do the tiniest of victories, and getting up in the morning every day and keeping going is a tiny victory.

Was there ever a time when you met someone and just knew instantly if you were going to like them or not? Circle Yes or No.

Something that scares me is _____. When I was a kid, some of the things that I did to pass the time were _____, _____, _____, and _____.

Exercise Explanation

Your ego is made up of your desires and other things that you consider a part of who you are. This exercise made you list some of these desires and things that are part of you. After doing this exercise, you got to know your ego just a little bit more. Getting to know every possible aspect of yourself allows you to find target areas that need improvement. It's very possible that your ego is in check and that it's your unconscious where the issue lies.

This exercise also allowed you to get to know your personal unconscious by thinking back to your childhood. We often don't think about memories from our childhood as they are repressed. While doing this exercise, you had to think back to that time and therefore explore your personal unconscious. You had to think about either a time when you were most happy or a time when you were miserable. Whichever the case may be, it allowed you to explore an aspect of yourself that may be out of balance and need some self-reflection.

Your collective unconscious, however, entails more of a societal aspect. When we think back to what we did as children, we often realize that many other people the same age did the same things. That is because what we did as children is what society says children should be doing. When listing off essential daily tasks, you begin to realize that it is also the society that tells us that those are essential daily tasks, and we do them without thinking. The reason is that they are a part of our collective unconscious.

Why? How Will This Help?

This exercise helps you to understand your ego, your personal unconscious, and your collective unconscious to know yourself better. It's only after reviewing the blueprints of how and why something works that anyone can see where something is going wrong. The fact that we need to review the blueprints could be why we are so curious and love a good mystery. People naturally want to know how, and this exercise helps you explore just that. Go forward and analyze yourself.

Moving Forward

First, you learned how to use the four main archetypes to analyze the source of a problem. After linking the source to a problem, you can devise a solution for going forward and ultimately eliminating the problem. The second thing you did was to identify your triggers, which are the emotional responses your unconscious was giving you to alert you of a problem. After analyzing your triggers, you were able to devise what the problem ultimately really was. Now, moving forward, you can repeat these two exercises daily to help eliminate any anxiety or negativity that surfaces. It's the third thing that you did, which was to do the exercise to understand your reality, that will ultimately give you a further understanding of your authentic self/ shadow self. The next step would be to go a bit further and explore your four main archetypes deeper.

The Self

This archetype is the part of our personality that interacts directly with our ego. The Self lies within the center of our personality and is surrounded by three other things. These three things that surround the Self are your consciousness, your ego, and your unconscious mind. They interact with the Self and are what give it life.

Your consciousness is composed of your points of view, beliefs, feelings, and thoughts. The source of why they exist is directly linked to the four main archetypes. It's the interaction of your consciousness, the ego, and the subconscious that make the self what it is. While they are interacting, aspects of your personality are formed. The ego, on the other hand, is formed from the moment of birth.

Your ego is your desire for survival, pleasure, success, achievements, or power. On our most basic primal level, we all want to stay to live another day. Even on our darkest days, filled with despair, we seek pleasure and to feel good. No matter how bad things get, your ego won't let you give up and wallow in your anxiety or negativity. Your ego desires success and achievement. It even searches for any level of power or control it can get its hands on because that's the way we are wired.

Your unconsciousness is all the aspects of your ego and your consciousness, but the ones that you're not aware of. The desire for power and control may be discussed with you; therefore, it gets repressed and it becomes an aspect of your unconsciousness. It's crucial to keep in mind that the fact that you repressed something does not make it go away. When dealing with anxiety or negativity, you might try to repress or overshadow these feelings. Pressing these feelings may give the appearance that you're not feeling them, but you are. All things that you repressed become a part of your unconscious mind and will indubitably affect you. To self-improve yourself, it is best to confront all aspects of yourself and repress nothing, or at least as much as you can.

The Shadow

Other things you may have repressed are ideas you may have had. All repressed ideas become a characteristic of your Shadow archetype. Along with repressed ideas are your weaknesses, desires, instincts, and shortcomings. Exploring this archetype will allow you to be your full self, both good and bad. It's only through acknowledging and working on our shortcomings that we can be our best selves. It's important to bring anything repressed to the surface during this self-exploration during the Shadow Plan.

Some possible repressed ideas might be that you should stop being someone's friend, and it would emerge through illogical irritation with them. You might not want to be this person's friend because they don't put the same amount of effort into the relationship as you. Because it doesn't seem realistic, you repress it, even though it quite possibly could be very healthy. Another possible repressed idea is about all the different types of desserts you want to bake and eat. You know that eating a lot of them is bad; therefore, you repress the idea. The good thing is that once this repressed idea comes to the surface, you can execute it with moderation. It is quite healthy to try a new baking recipe every weekend or every other weekend. While bringing these repressed ideas to the surface, it is important to acknowledge your weaknesses as well.

If you know that after baking a cake, you will eat all of it because it is one of your weaknesses, you can plan accordingly. If eating too many desserts is a weakness, you can invite friends over to share your cake with you after you bake it. By knowing you're going to share the cake with others, you conquer your weakness. Another possible weakness could be that you get easily bored; therefore, you find it difficult to do the repetitive tasks of the day. Once you know this is a weakness, then you can endeavor to make them more interesting by listening to music or doing multiple tasks at once. Another way to conquer a weakness is by rewarding yourself with one of your desires.

A desire that you could reward yourself with is a nice treat like a candy bar or a Caesar salad. When eating foods that you like, your body releases pleasure hormones as well anytime you indulge your desires. When you hang out with your friends and you're laughing and having a good time, pleasure hormones are also released, as you dive into this desire. If you find physical activities pleasurable because of this desire, your body will also release pleasure hormones. Knowing this, one can conclude that anything our body releases pleasure hormones for is one of our desires. Our body does this through instinct to incentivize us to do things that we like.

Instincts play an important role in our daily lives, as well as the Shadow archetype. Jung believed that there were five basic human instincts, and they were as follows: creativity, reflection, activity, sexuality, and hunger. Creativity is defined as the ability to create things that are original; we all have a desire for this. This instinct may emerge through the desire for children or through the simple aspiration to create art. Instead, the instinct for reflection can emerge through the belief in one's soul or desire to express thoughts and feelings. Moreover, your instinct for activity is merely a desire for work to help your society or group of people. Finally, sexuality as an instinct is not so easily explained, because it has many components. It can be your desire for another human being or how your specific sex fits in within society. Wanting to eat and craving to devour both knowledge and sustenance is another basic instinct. All of these instincts are characteristic of your Shadow archetype as well as any perceived shortcomings.

You may find yourself physically not as fit as others, and that might be a perceived shortcoming. It's also possible that you don't learn concepts as fast as others, which could be another example. While it is true that an abundance of perceived shortcomings can lead to anxiety and negativity, it is important to know why you view them as such. Your anxiety and negativity may be a direct result of a problem within your unconscious mind. Whether they hold true or not, shortcomings are characteristic of your Shadow archetype. Therefore, all proceed shortcomings must be addressed and/or faced.

Other things you must face are any feelings of envy, greed, prejudice, or hate you may have. These feelings cloud and taint the Shadow archetype, and you must face and overcome them for the purpose of self-improvement. Having these characteristics will undoubtedly create negativity and anxiety because of the imbalance within yourself.

Many of these characteristics may indeed reside in your unconscious, which results in difficulty facing and overcoming them. If they are within your unconscious mind, they will emerge in your dreams or possibly even visions. These characteristics could even come out as unusual feelings during an event or occurrence of some kind. While you classify them as atypical, they are occurring for a reason, and through self-reflection or exploration of your authentic self, those reasons will become apparent.

The Anima

The Anima archetype is also apparent and easily explored. Anything that you see, or others see about yourself that is an anomaly becomes a part of the Anima archetype. While it's true that we live in an age of enlightenment, it is also true that we have certain characteristics that decidedly are male and female. If we display characteristics of the opposite sex that we believe we should have, it becomes a part of our Anima archetype. Something as simple as an extraordinarily tall female can be a part of the Anima archetype. Because of this anomaly, we will compensate and behave differently, whether we are doing it consciously or subconsciously. Really, any social influences that counter our self-image can also be a part of our Anima archetype.

Some social influences that might counter your self-image might be that you're a bigger male and dress like you're tough, and you don't have strong emotions. There is no direct link between someone's size and how they dress or between how someone dresses and how they feel. Despite that, society has created stereotypes, and it is those stereotypes that shape your Anima archetype. Society also helps shape your Persona archetype, except this archetype is there to protect us from stereotypes.

The Persona

The mask we wear around our family and friends is to meet standards and to give off an outward appearance that we meet those standards. We will look people in the eyes when we're talking to them so that they feel heard. It doesn't matter that we saw something out of the corner of our eye that we want to look at. The Persona archetype compels us to make our friends and family feel heard by making eye contact. When you're planning to go to a party, you will inevitably take extra care of your hygiene. You're what the Persona archetype dictates because everyone else will do this, so you must do it as well to fit in and meet the standard. Even if our desire is to let loose and just go in something nice, we will be compelled not to. Your Persona that you show to others will not allow you to do anything else without feeling anxious or having negative thoughts towards yourself.

EXERCISE: MY FOUR MAIN ARCHETYPES!

Think about a time when you were anxious or negative and use the four main archetypes to postulate why that may be. List one or two things about your Self, Shadow, Anima, and Persona archetypes below.

THE SELF

1) _____
   _____
2) _____
   _____

THE SHADOW

1) _____
   _____
2) _____
   _____

THE ANIMA

1) _____
   _____
2) _____
   _____

THE PERSONA

1) _____
   _____
2) _____
   _____

Exercise Explanation

Doing this exercise will help you analyze your negativity and/or your anxiety. The four main archetypes or the cause of a problem can be a tool for you. Knowing your authentic self is the only way to do any self-improvement. Analyzing your desires will allow you to see where they're not being fulfilled. If you know where your perceived shortcomings are, you can adjust accordingly. After completing this exercise, you can construct a plan to eliminate both your negativity and your anxiety.

Why? How Will This Help?

The source of your negativity and your anxiety can only be found through self-analysis. If you want to not feel anxiety, you must eliminate what you're anxious about. If you want to stop feeling so negative about yourself, you must know why. You can construct a plan only after you have all the information. This exercise allows you to obtain that very information.

Keep It Positive

While doing all of this self-analysis and exercises, it's important to stay positive, so doing a gratitude exercise would be advisable. There are things that you can say to yourself to stay positive. As well as positive, there are actions that you can do that will help keep yourself positive and recharge your emotional batteries. It can be helpful for you to stay positive to start off the day with an uplifting statement. It can also be beneficial to have a mantra that you repeat to yourself throughout the day.

Things You Can Say

Something you can tell yourself once you wake up is, "It's a new day, and it's going to be a good one!" This allows you to start over and get away from anything that might be bringing you down from the day before. Saying this is going to give you motivation. You could also say to yourself throughout the day, "I am strong, and I can do this!"

Reminding yourself that you are strong affirms that you are strong enough to conquer anything and that you can achieve your goal. Saying, "You can do this," reinforces what you already know in your heart. We all need reminders, which is why doing this enables you to reach your goal.

Things That You Can Do

Reminders can be very helpful, but after you remind yourself that you can do it, you got to do it. Doing exercises to keep yourself positive gives you the energy and motivation to get things done. Going for an occasional walk in the woods can help you see the beauty in the world and show that it's worth it to keep going. It's easy to get caught up in all the negativity in the world, and a beautiful reminder that there's still good in it can be beneficial. Text someone that you're close to and have a nice conversation. In the morning, drink a cup of coffee and focus on every sip and the warmth when it touches your tongue. Being in each moment and cherishing every second that you enjoy is yet another thing that you can do to remain positive. If you're up for it, think back to a time when things were worse and cherish where you are now. Even doing a gratitude exercise every 2 to 3 days can help keep you positive and motivated to continue your self-improvement journey.

Here is a gratitude exercise that you could try. The first thing you do is take a deep breath and clear your mind. Then, try to think of ten things that you are grateful for and you feel like they are making your life better. Write down something that brings you joy and that you're thankful that you have. Is there someone in your life that's really been there for you? Write down the name of the person that's been there for you. You could even be grateful for an experience that you had; it helped you.

EXERCISE: GRATITUDE

List 15 things that you are grateful for:

1) _____

2) _____

3) _____

4) _____

5) _____

7) _____

8) _____

9) _____

10) _____

11) _____

12) _____

13) _____

14) _____

15) _____

A LOVELY THING

Write more about one of the things from your gratitude list, and dig into the ways this thing makes your life better.

_____

_____

_____

_____

_____

_____

_____

_____

_____

_____

_____

_____

_____

_____

_____

_____

_____

_____

_____

_____

Exercise Explanation

Writing down the things that you are grateful for will bring them to the forefront of your mind. While it's true that unconsciously, you are always thankful for them, it's important to bring them to your conscious mind. Sometimes we just need a reminder of things that we are grateful for so that we can feel the joy. Life can get in the way, and we can get consumed by our anxiety or negativity. This exercise helps push those feelings aside so that we can feel grateful again.

Why? How Will This Help Me?

After this exercise, you should feel a sense of joy and happiness. Even a moment of relief from our anxiety or negativity is beneficial. This exercise helps give you a break from feeling your anxiety or negativity. Hold on to this feeling of happiness and let it motivate you to eliminate your anxiety and negativity.

GETTING READY TO USE
THE WORKBOOK

You have already chosen to make those self-improvements and eliminate your anxiety or negativity. The next step is to get into the right mindset for self-improvement, and for eliminating those feelings. Complete your Shadow Plan with an open mind and be curious about yourself. There is hope, so be optimistic that you will succeed. You can do it. Believe, truly believe, that you will be able to do this, and you will. Remember, there are things that not even you know about yourself. Don't be afraid to explore the unknown about yourself and have your point of view changed.

When you're beginning, your journey of self-improvement is a good idea to have clear goals and know where you want to end up. Keep a clear goal in mind while doing your Shadow Plan. It can be helpful to imagine what your life will be like without any anxiety or negativity. That's why doing this Dear Future Me exercise can really help you know what your clear goal is.

EXERCISE: DEAR FUTURE ME

Write a workbook entry detailing things you want your future self to have. Consider what your future will look like without any anxiety or negativity. Don't be afraid to be ambiguous and optimistic with your vision. Being a dreamer and wanting things for yourself allows you to get more out of life.

Dear Future Me,

_____

_____

_____

_____

_____

_____

_____

_____

_____

_____

_____

_____

_____

_____

_____

_____

_____

Sincerely Myself Now,

_____

_____

_____

_____

_____

_____

_____

_____

Exercise Explanation

Writing a letter to your future self allows you to imagine where you can be. Looking into the future can help you realize what your goals are and where you want to go. Doing this exercise will also help affirm that you can get there. You are on an ongoing journey and knowing that there is hope at the end waiting for you helps keep you motivated.

Why? How Will This Help Me?

You can't make any progress if you think you can't. You also can't eliminate that anxiety or negativity if you can't imagine life without it. Completing this exercise helps you imagine just that. It also helps you make your dream a reality because to get instructions during your journey, you need to have a destination.

PROMPTS FOR SHADOW WORK & SELF-DISCOVERY

EXPLORING THE DEPTHS

In this journal, you will find a series of exercises that will guide you in discovering your inner shadow and help you overcome your personal limits. However, to achieve these results, you will need to commit constantly and dedicate time every day to face your fears and insecurities.

You will be able to recognize and manage your emotions, understand your behaviors, and be come the best version of yourself. Remember that each exercise will take you deeper, confronting strong emotions and intense sensations, so always be aware of who you are now and why you have chosen to embark on this journey.

Take this path seriously and approach it in the way that you deem most appropriate and correct. Only then can you achieve the results you seek and improve your inner life. Your commitment and dedication will lead to significant changes in your life, just as it has for many others.

THE CLUTTER IN YOUR MIND

Think about when your house is a mess. Your stuff is thrown all around the floor, stacked up in haphazard piles. To find anything, you need to dig through all the piles until you find what you need. In the process, you end up making more of a mess, and the more mess you have, the harder it becomes to declutter because you don't even know where to start! The same is true of your mind. Like your house, your brain can easily get cluttered with a lot of negative and warped thoughts. These thoughts can confuse you and make it hard to be your fullest self.

Today, you will start a process of spring cleaning by beginning to differentiate clutter from meaningful thoughts and beliefs you have. Generally speaking, you can identify clutter by finding what parts of your life make you feel stressed or anxious.

What Clutter Do You Have?

Take a few minutes to write about the clutter in your life that makes it hard for you to function as well as you would like.

_____

_____

_____

_____

_____

_____

_____

_____

_____

_____

_____

_____

_____

_____

_____

_____

What Clutter Do You Have?

Take a few minutes to write about the clutter in your life that makes it hard for you to function as well as you would like.

1. _____
2. _____
3. _____
4. _____
5. _____
6. _____
7. _____
8. _____
9. _____
10. _____

BEING VULNERABLE

Vulnerability is the only way you can have deeper connections with other people. It is all about being honest about who you are, and that includes being honest about all the parts of yourself you'd rather hide. You don't have to share everything with everyone, but being more open can help reduce any shame you feel.

When were You Vulnerable?

Discuss a time when you were vulnerable. What happened? How did you feel? What risks were you taking? What was your reward? What fears or doubts did you have?

_____

_____

_____

_____

_____

_____

_____

_____

_____

_____

THE SHADOW AND STRESS

The shadow self takes any negative stress you have and magnifies it with the stress of the past. When you get stuck in your head, and the stress is building up, it signals that you have some level of disconnect with your own internal world. By taking some time to process what is happening within, you can overcome some of your negative stress.

Today I Was Stressed

Write about a time today or in the past week when stress has nega - tively impacted you. What events surrounded that stress, and how did you try to deal with what you were feeling?

_____

_____

_____

_____

_____

_____

_____

_____

_____

_____

FACING YOUR FEARS

No matter how strong or resilient you are, you cannot escape fear. Fear is a vital part of human nature because it is an alert that something might be wrong, and it prepares your body to respond promptly to potential dangers that may arise. No, it's not fun, but your fear is something engrained in you to promote survival. It is something you need to survive.

Much of the shadow self is fear, and your fears can be so deeply buried that you lose track of their root. It is by facing your fears that you can overcome them and become more resilient in the face of challenges. Listening to your fear is a fantastic tool, but you cannot let it run your life. If you do, you make your life smaller when you could be making it bigger.

Fear Inventory

This fear inventory can help you identify them and their purpose.

I am afraid of _____ because of the following reasons:

_____

_____

_____

This fear causes me to _____,

_____, and _____

_____. I know this fear has a purpose, but

I want to _____ even though I'm

scared. When I finally face all the fears I have, I want to _____

_____

Fear Memory

Describe a moment when you felt a lot of fear. Tell your story however you see fit.

_____

_____

_____

_____

_____

_____

_____

_____

_____

_____

_____

_____

_____

_____

_____

_____

_____

_____

_____

_____

_____

_____

TUG OF WAR WITHIN YOU

Internal conflicts are the number one thing to lead to indecision. When you don't know what to do in a situation, it's often because you are battling two parts of yourself. Often, your shadow self is the stronger force and may lead to you making decisions that protect the things you are ashamed of rather than boosting the things that make you proud.

Internal War

Imagine that there's a war happening within your brain. What does this war look like? Who are the parties involved? What are the stakes? Use these questions to shape your response, but feel free to imagine beyond these questions.

_____

_____

_____

_____

_____

_____

_____

_____

_____

_____

DEALING WITH TRAUMA

The traumatized brain acts differently, and it can become fixated on the trauma rather than the present. It comes in many forms, but no matter the type of trauma you have, it likely has a big impact on your life, even if you aren't initially aware of how much it may influence you. Today, you will learn to unpack your trauma and start to understand the major life events that your shadow self may try to suppress to protect you from negative feelings.

Even if you don't think of yourself as having trauma, you should reflect on the biggest obstacles you have endured in your life, which every person experiences to some extent. Furthermore, many people minimalize their experiences, but to deal with them, you have to confront and begin to process all the things that have made your life tumble off balance and have shaped your view of the world.

Trauma in Your Body

How does your trauma make your body feel? Think about the physical sensations that the hardest parts of your life have on you and the way your body remembers what you have been through.

_____

_____

_____

_____

_____

NURTURE YOUR INNER CHILD

Nurturing your inner child is a powerful practice that allows you to reconnect with the innocent, curious, and playful aspects of yourself. When you nurture your inner child, you provide a safe and loving space for that part of you to express its needs, desires, and emotions. Close your eyes and imagine a beautiful garden, filled with vibrant colors and delightful sounds. As you explore this garden, you come across a small, shy child. This child is your inner child, longing for your attention and care. Sit with the child, hold their hand, and listen to what they have to say.

Write a letter to your inner child, assuring them that they are loved, protected, and deserving of joy and happiness.

_____

_____

_____

_____

_____

_____

_____

_____

_____

_____

_____

_____

SHOWING EMPATHY

When you become driven by the shadow-self, you may become overly self-consumed and lose sight of how others are feeling. You may project how you feel about yourself onto others. A person who hates their impulsive nature may see someone else with that same trait and treat that person harshly. However, when you confront your shadow self, you can instead show empathy to other people with those same traits. In turn, you will build a path towards showing empathy to yourself for the traits you don't like about yourself.

Missed Chances

Write about a time you didn't show someone compassion but wished you did. How would you do things differently? Why did you not show compassion in that moment?

_____

_____

_____

_____

_____

_____

_____

_____

_____

WINDING DOWN

When you are a busy person, winding down can be the hardest part of the day. Your mind may feel like it just won't shut off. That's normal because the world often prioritizes getting stuff done, and with that mindset, the negative and fearful nature of your shadow self can take over and make you too worried to calm your mind. While winding down is most commonly associated with just before you sleep, it's a process that can be useful anytime your mind feels overly busy. For example, maybe you're in the middle of a hectic work project. Taking a second to wind down can help you reorient so that you can be more productive. Finding internal peace gives you a sense of calmness and well-being.

The Chaos in My Mind

Reflect on a difficult moment you have had today. Discuss why this moment was so hard and why it felt so challenging to you. Think about what you can do going forward.

_____

_____

_____

_____

_____

_____

_____

_____

_____

_____

_____

_____

_____

_____

How I feel So Far

Think about how you have been feeling lately. How has this changed from how you felt in the past? What's been bothering you? What has made you feel good?

_____

_____

_____

_____

_____

_____

_____

_____

_____

_____

_____

INNER PEACE BREATHING

The way you breathe can impact the way you feel and how much your shadow self will impact your decisions. By learning to stop and breathe deeply, you can fuel your mind and your soul. Whenever you're starting to feel stressed or overwhelmed, take a moment to stop and focus on your breathing. All this requires is for you to inhale, hold for four seconds and then exhale for four seconds. If you do this for even just five minutes, you can start to feel a difference in your mental state. Inner-peace breathing means giving yourself time away from the chaos, and by taking this time, you can do other things more efficiently because you can use more of your brain to tackle hard tasks, making it faster in the long run.

Post breathing Reflection

After you have taken a chance to breathe through the chaos of your life, reflect on how you felt before breathing and how you felt after you breathed. Noticing these changes can help you see the power of breathing.

_____
_____
_____
_____
_____
_____
_____

SENSORY GROUNDING

When life gets difficult, it's easy to become overwhelmed by the sensory stimuli around you. However, while your senses can overwhelm you, you can also use them to ground you. Grounding practices are common in many types of therapies, and they are simple for any person to apply. If you are feeling disconnected or detached, you can use sensory grounding to get back to a healthy emotional baseline. This process begins by identifying three things you can see, three things you can hear, and three things you feel. You then repeat this process with two things and then do it one more time with one thing.

For example, imagine you are in a bedroom. Your sensory grounding may look like this.

ROUND 1

See

1.   Sheets on your bed

2.   Your pile of laundry

3.   A picture on the wall

Hear

1.   Ticking of clock

2.   Air conditioning

3.   Kids playing outside

Feel

1.   Your duvet

2.   Phone under your fingers

3.   Foot against your other foot

ROUND 2

See

1.   A decorative pillow

2.   Your desk

Hear

1.   Birds tweeting

2.   Music from the next room

Feel

1.   Cool air blowing on you

2.   Weight on your lap from your pet

ROUND 3

See

1.   Your favorite chair in the corner

Hear

1.   The TV blaring

Feel

1.   A fuzzy blanket on your legs

You can repeat this process wherever you are and whenever you need to calm yourself down. After you have practiced your grounding exercise, reflect on your feelings. How did you feel before grounding yourself with your senses, and how do you feel after grounding yourself?

VISUALIZE WHAT YOU WANT

Visualization allows you to use creative tools to create the outcomes you want. When you visualize, you imagine the things you want to happen, and you can do so as creatively as you want. The more vivid, the better. Visualization teaches your unconscious brain what to prioritize, and the mental images you create stick in your mind. For example, if you're stressed, you can imagine your stress is a big balloon. Imagine the air going into the balloon is all the things bothering you. Then, imagine popping the balloon with a long pin. All the things stressing you come rushing out, and the weight on your shoulders falls off with the gust of wind.

Ambition Visualization

Imagine one of your ambitions as vividly as you can. Write about it here.

_____

_____

_____

_____

_____

_____

_____

_____

_____

_____

MINDFULNESS BEGINS NOW

Mindfulness is the process of being more aware of what is currently happening in your body, mind, and the world around you. While many people think mindfulness is just meditation, it is so much more. You can be mindful in all areas of your life, such as eating, exercise, and work. When you are mindful, you don't try to get rid of your thoughts, and you don't try to shut out your shadow self; rather, you focus on how you can listen to those voices without judgment. Remember that thoughts alone do not make you moral or immoral, and good people can have "bad" thoughts, and by learning to not linger on these thoughts, you take off some pressure from yourself.

What's Happening Around You?

Take a moment to write about your surroundings and the thoughts you are having right now. Don't linger on any one thought for too long. Let the thoughts flow organically and pay attention to your senses.

_____

_____

_____

_____

_____

_____

_____

MEDITATION MINUTES

Meditation is a useful technique that challenges you to sit in a peaceful place for several minutes. During this time, you focus on the sensations in your body and imagine energy flowing through you. For example, you can imagine that there is light spreading through your body. This light goes in through your head, and it exits your extremities. When you can think in this way, you begin to feel calm. This calmness follows you into moments of stress, allowing you to be more resilient.

Try your first meditation without trying too hard, take it as a new experience to understand your thoughts.

Post Mediation Reflection

After meditating, take some time to reflect on your experience.

Before meditation I felt:

_____

_____

_____

_____

During meditation I felt:

_____

_____

_____

_____

After meditation I felt:

_____

_____

_____

_____

What thoughts reoccurred during meditation:

_____

_____

_____

_____

What did I observe during meditation:

_____

_____

_____

_____

Other thoughts related to meditation:

_____

_____

_____

_____

_____

_____

MAKING MANTRAS

Mantras are statements you use to encourage yourself and redirect yourself when you are struggling. They are usually short so that you can repeat them often. An example of a mantra is, "I can get through this with the strength of my character." You can make a mantra for anything and use it in any situation.

My Mantras

Write seven mantras. They can be related to whatever areas of your life you want. Feel free to write extras as well.

1. _____

_____

_____

_____

2. _____

_____

_____

_____

3. _____

_____

_____

_____

4. _____

_____

_____

_____

5. _____

_____

_____

_____

6. _____

_____

_____

_____

7. _____

_____

_____

_____

REWRITING YOUR THOUGHTS

Your nasty thoughts may convince you that you can't or you shouldn't do certain things. These thoughts are often built upon faulty foundations, which is why you need to address them and start to rewrite any thought that is keeping you from being your genuine self.

Thought Transformation

In this exercise, you will learn to take a negative thought and make it into a positive one.

Example:

Scenario: You are stuck as you work on a project. You don't know what to do next.

Negative Thought: "I am stupid."

Thought Transformation: "I am unaware of the best practices to use for this project, but I have the skills required to do some additional research and ask for extra help when needed."

Now, you can try it for yourself!

Scenario:

_____
_____
_____

Negative Thought:

_____
_____
_____

Thought Transformation:

_____
_____
_____

Negative thoughts list

Write about ten negative thoughts that you would like to change. After you have chosen them repeat the exercise.

1. _____
2. _____
3. _____
4. _____
5. _____
6. _____
7. _____
8. _____
9. _____
10. _____

MIRROR, MIRROR ON THE WALL

If you have a bad relationship with your shadow self, it's common to have a distorted sense of self-image. This self-image can refer to how you see yourself physically and how you see yourself internally. In any case, disconnection from the shadow can increase your self-doubts, and you can start to see everything you are in a negative light. You start to feel like something is wrong with you, and your eyes can even fool you when you look in the mirror. It's time to take back your self-image and find the good qualities in your reflection.

What Do I See?

Stand in front of the mirror and write about what you see. Once you have dealt with your physical self, go deeper and try to determine what you "see" within yourself. Try to look into your eyes without looking away and try to understand what you feel.

Are you afraid? Look away? Do you know the person you are looking at in the mirror?

_____

_____

_____

_____

RECLAIMING PAST TRAUMAS

Reclaiming past traumas is a brave and transformative journey towards healing and self-empowerment. Acknowledging the impact of past traumas allows you to release their hold on your present life and create space for growth and resilience. Close your eyes and imagine yourself standing at the edge of a vast ocean. Each wave that crashes onto the shore represents a past trauma. With each wave, visualize yourself gathering the strength and courage to face and process that trauma. Feel the power of the ocean within you, allowing it to wash away the pain and replace it with strength and resilience.

Write a letter to yourself, honoring the courage it takes to confront past traumas and affirming your commitment to your healing journey.

_____

_____

_____

_____

_____

_____

_____

_____

_____

_____

_____

_____

A LETTER TO LITTLE YOU

Your past self has been through a lot, and some of what they have been through could be things that you have inflicted on yourself. Getting in touch with the little version of yourself is an important part of your shadow work because this process emphasizes acknowledging what has happened in your past and the way we all have an inner child within us that represents all the past hurts, hopes, and everything else that we have repressed and shoved into the shadow.

Hello Little Me

Write a letter to your inner child.

_____

_____

_____

_____

_____

_____

_____

_____

_____

_____

_____

_____

_____

SHADOWY HABITS

Habits shape much of what you do each day. Think about your morning routine: that is a habit. A habit is like a shortcut that enables you to easily complete tasks you have done before without putting in so much mental effort. Habits are useful because they allow you to save your energy for other tasks, but not all habits are good for you. Some are driven by the subconscious hurting of the shadow. For example, someone who abuses substances may try to turn off their shadow self through numbing behaviors associated with certain substances. This habit seems appealing on some level because it gives emotional release, but in the long run, it is harmful. Awareness of shadow-driven habits can help you replace those bad habits with healthier ones.

My List of Habits

Write ten of your habits.

1. _____

2. _____

3. _____

4. _____

5. _____

6. _____

7. _____

8. _____

9. _____

10. _____

My Worst Habit

Think about your worst habit and the impact it has on your life. What habits could you choose to do instead of your worst habits?

_____

_____

_____

_____

_____

_____

_____

_____

_____

_____

_____

_____

_____

_____

_____

_____

_____

_____

_____

_____

CAREER TRACKS

It's time to reflect on your career and whether you are satisfied with your professional trajectory. Careers come with a lot of mixed feelings, and by reflecting on your own career, you can determine if your career is adequately serving your needs.

Career Inventory

Consider the following prompts about your career.

My favorite part of my career:

_____

_____

_____

_____

_____

My least favorite part of my career:

_____

_____

_____

_____

_____

How I felt about my career when I started versus how I feel about it now:

_____

_____

_____

_____

_____

_____

_____

Is my career a good fit for my present needs?

_____

_____

_____

_____

_____

_____

_____

Are there changes I could make to improve my relationship with career?

_____

_____

_____

_____

_____

_____

_____

FRIENDSHIP IS THE SPICE OF LIFE

Friendships are an important part of shadow work because this journey isn't something you need to go on alone. You don't need to have a lot of friends, but having at least one person you know is there for you is crucial. Having friends you can talk to and who can help you through hard moments is an invaluable tool. Additionally, looking at the patterns in your friendships can help you unpack elements of your shadow self. For example, you may tend to have anxious attachments to your friends because of struggles you had as a child. By addressing these parts of your relationships, you can improve your relationships and feel safer in friendships.

My Best Friend

Write about the closest friend you have or one of the closest friends you have. Talk about how they enrich your life. Think about the flaws in your relationship with this person and what tends to cause arguments.

_____

_____

_____

_____

_____

_____

_____

_____

FAMILY MATTERS

Family is no doubt one of the more complicated parts of life. Even if you have one of the best families, that doesn't mean your family is issue free! All families have struggles, and these struggles often reflect your shadow self because you learn certain messages as a child about how relationships and the world at large operate through your family.

Thus, thinking about the way your family operates, both past and present, can help you learn more about your shadow self and the fears that are buried within you. For instance, if a child has a neglectful parent, they may expect that kind of treatment in future relationships because that's what they learned is normal.

Family Tree

Write about some of the family members who have influenced you the most.

Family Member 1:

_____

_____

_____

_____

_____

_____

Family Member 2:

_____

_____

_____

_____

_____

Family Member 3:

_____

_____

_____

_____

_____

Family Member 4:

_____

_____

_____

_____

_____

FINDING PURPOSE

Life means very little if you don't have any purpose. Finding purpose is one of the core factors of feeling alive. Unfortunately, your shadow self can drive you away from your purpose and make you feel like you are unimportant and have no clearly defined future. While you cannot decide exactly what your future will be, that doesn't mean you cannot build towards what you want.

Imagine you are in the woods. You want to find something cool, but you don't know what that thing is; it can be pretty hard to find something you haven't defined, but if you know you want to find a special tree, you can use the information around you to point in the direction of the tree. There's always room for some spontaneity, but having some sense of purpose is a must.

I Contribute

Write the ways you contribute to various areas of your life.

Family

1. _____
2. _____
3. _____
4. _____
5. _____

Friends

1. _____
2. _____
3. _____
4. _____
5. _____

Work/School/Occupational Activities

1. _____
2. _____
3. _____
4. _____
5. _____

MY purpose is To...

What is that you are meant to do? Think big, and don't be afraid to think about your ideal role in the world.

_____

_____

_____

_____

_____

_____

_____

_____

_____

_____

_____

_____

_____

_____

_____

_____

_____

_____

This is Me Trying

After you have tried something new today, think about how that new thing made you feel. Did it feel good? Did it create any distress? Would you try it again?

_____

_____

_____

_____

_____

_____

_____

_____

_____

_____

_____

_____

_____

_____

_____

_____

_____

_____

_____

FIVE YEARS FROM NOW

Thinking about where you want to be five years from now can help you do shadow work that propels you to where you want to be.

My Life in Five Years

Write about what you want your life to be five years from now. Make it as imaginative as you'd like. Don't hesitate to have big dreams.

_____

_____

_____

_____

_____

_____

_____

_____

_____

_____

_____

_____

_____

_____

LOVE OF MY LIFE

Think about the kind of romantic relationship you want to have. Romance is not necessary for you to thrive, but if it is important to you, you have to consider how your shadow self impacts your relationships.

What I want

Circle some qualities you want in a relationship. You may want many of these things, but choose the five that most appeal to you.

Compassion

Intelligence

Stability

Communication

Conversation

Gifts

Kindness

Growth

Physical safety

Gentleness

Adventures

Passion

Vulnerability

Security

Depth

Intimacy

Romance

Travel

Excitement

Spontaneity

Sharing meals

Emotional connection

Spirituality

Laughter

Physical attraction

Love

Sex

Grand gestures

Shared hobbies

Physical activities

Procreation

Physical affection

Reassurance

Care

My Past Relationships

Talk about past or current relationships, and focus on one relationship that had or has the most impact.

_____
_____
_____
_____
_____
_____
_____
_____
_____
_____
_____
_____
_____
_____
_____
_____
_____
_____
_____
_____

AFFIRMATIONS FOR SHADOW INTEGRATION

SHADOW AFFIRMATIONS

Integrating the parts of ourselves that we have rejected or hidden can be a challenging and painful process, but it can also be incredibly liberating. When we accept all aspects of ourselves, including those that make us feel vulnerable or insecure, we can feel more whole and complete. The following affirmations can help support your shadow integration process and help you develop a loving and compassionate attitude towards yourself.

Before delving into the affirmations, it is important to understand how they can help with shadow integration. These affirmations are designed to help you:

• Accept and integrate all parts of yourself, including those that you may have rejected or hidden in the past.

• Develop a positive and empowering mindset that supports your growth and transformation.

• Replace old patterns of thought and behavior with new, healthier ones.

Self-Love

- *I am worthy of love and acceptance, regardless of my imperfections.*
- *I love and accept myself fully, with all my parts.*
- *I am the source of my love and happiness, and I give myself permission to cultivate them within me.*
- *I choose to love myself unconditionally, without judgment or criticism.*
- *I give myself permission to heal past wounds and love myself again.*

Self-Confidence

- I am secure and confident in myself, regardless of the challenges that may arise.
- I give myself permission to explore new experiences and make positive choices in my life.
- I am able to make conscious decisions and trust my instincts.
- I am able to overcome my fears and face challenges with courage and determination.
- I give myself permission to follow my heart and pursue my dreams, even if they seem unreasonable.

Shadow Acceptance

- I welcome my shadow as part of me and integrate it into my life.
- I am able to accept my negative emotions without judgment or criticism.
- I give myself permission to explore my less-known sides and accept them without fear.
- I am able to see the beauty and value in all parts of myself, including those I may have rejected in the past.
- I accept my vulnerability and fragility as part of my humanity.

Emotional Healing

- I am able to heal from past emotional wounds and let them go.
- I give myself permission to freely express my emotions and accept them as part of me.
- I am able to forgive myself and others for any past mistakes.
- I welcome my sadness and pain without judgment or criticism.
- I am able to transform my negative emotions into opportunities for growth and change.

Self-Esteem

- I give myself permission to appreciate my worth and uniqueness.
- I am able to see the good in myself and others, even when things seem difficult.
- I welcome my flaws and imperfections, knowing they make me unique and special.
- I am able to express myself authentically and genuinely, without fear of judgment.
- I give myself permission to take control of my life and make positive choices for my well-being.

Personal Transformation

- I am able to change and grow at any point in my life.
- I give myself permission to explore new possibilities and experience life in different ways.
- I am able to embrace my uniqueness and appreciate my differences.
- I accept my mistakes as part of my growth and learning.
- I am able to find inner peace and happiness through the acceptance and integration of all parts of myself.

Compassion and Kindness

- I am kind and compassionate with myself, regardless of my imperfections.
- I give myself permission to take care of myself and dedicate the necessary time to my well-being.
- I am able to see the good in others and treat them with kindness and respect.
- I welcome my fragility and vulnerability without judgment or criticism.
- I give myself permission to be empathetic and help others when they need it.

Gratitude

- I am grateful for all the experiences that have brought me to this point in my life.
- I give myself permission to appreciate the small things in life and find beauty in the everyday.
- I am able to find gratitude even in difficult and painful situations.
- I welcome gratitude as part of my daily well-being practice.
- I am grateful for the loved ones in my life and their support and love.

Mindfulness

- I am present in the present moment and aware of my thoughts, emotions, and sensations.
- I give myself permission to slow down and enjoy the present without worries about the past or future.
- I am able to observe my thoughts and emotions without judgment or criticism.
- I welcome mindfulness as part of my daily well-being practice.
- I am able to find inner peace through the practice of mindfulness.

Authenticity

- I am authentic and true to myself and others.
- I give myself permission to express myself authentically, even when things seem difficult.
- I am able to embrace my authenticity and live according to my values and beliefs.
- I welcome authenticity as part of my identity and well-being.
- I am able to find happiness and satisfaction in life through authentic expression of myself.

How to Use the Affirmations

To get the most out of these affirmations, try reciting them daily, both in the morning and at night. You can also write them in a journal or repeat them mentally throughout the day. When reciting these affirmations, try to embody the feelings and emotions behind them, and visualize yourself fully embracing all parts of yourself.

Additionally, it can be helpful to reflect on any resistance or discomfort that arises while reciting these affirmations. This resistance may be an indication of areas where you need to focus on healing and integrating your shadow aspects.

Remember that this is a journey, and it may take time and effort to fully integrate all parts of yourself. But with patience, self-compassion, and consistent practice, you can cultivate a more loving and accepting relationship with yourself, and experience greater peace and fulfillment in your life.

MY 21 DAYS
SHADOW PLAN

"What you are you do not see.
What you see is your shadow."

- Rabindranath Tagore -

This Shadow Plan will give you a full understanding of how to construct your 21-day plan. You will learn how to select daily exercises and create goals. There are even instructions on what type of mindset you should have going into this endeavor. It's completely understandable if you don't quite comprehend what a Shadow Plan is even supposed to be. This section will answer all your possible questions.

What Is a Shadow Plan?

A Shadow Plan is a plan to explore your shadow self and get to know your inner child. While using your Shadow Plan, you'll be analyzing your four main archetypes. You will be using this plan with a series of steps to ultimately eliminate your anxiety and negativity through understanding. This is a blueprint for analyzing yourself by yourself.

How to Make a Shadow Plan?

The first step to making a shadow plan is to come up with a daily routine to analyze yourself. You will create a plan not only to analyze yourself but to postulate possible solutions. After formulating a solution, it will be your duty to implement it in your daily life. You're doing all this in the name of eliminating your negativity and anxiety using these tools. The daily exercises are your tools, as is the information contained in this Shadow Workbook. Choose three exercises from the exercise choices and come up with a daily plan to do them. These exercise choices are listed below in the shadow exercise choices section following this one. Every 2 to 3 days, do one of the gratitude exercises given to you in both the Shadow Plan exercise section and within the Workbook's content. Through your dedication and commitment to achieving your clear goals, you will make a plan.

How Will I Benefit from the Plan?

Completing the plan will enable you to live a fuller life with a more joyful and positive outlook on life. After using the Shadow Plan, you can continue to use the tools that you have learned to go further in your journey of self-improvement. With more improvement, more joy will come into your life and to those around you.

What's the Purpose of the Shadow Plan?

The purpose of the Shadow Plan is for you to improve yourself and your quality of life. It will give you the opportunity of a better life and a better self. If you have anxiety and or negativity, this Shadow Plan will help you get rid of it. It will help you find problems at their source. After doing this, this plan will help you find solutions. In conclusion, the purpose of this Shadow Workbook is to make your life better.

LET'S GET IT DONE

Now let's start constructing your Shadow Plan. Look back at the exercise choices section and look over all five of the exercises. While you do, find one that would fit into your morning routine. The first exercise, the Meditation Reflection Exercise, is a good choice to do in the morning because you can do it on the way to work. For the Shadow Plan to be most effective and easier on you, it's important to be able to do these exercises every day for the next 21 days. Keep that in mind while making it.

Next, select an exercise that you can do periodically during the day. The exercise that you might find the easiest to do during the day is exercise number three. The trigger log exercise can be done in a notebook that you keep near you or on your person. The trigger reflection can even be done later when you are on a break while you're at work. As you go about your day, pay attention to your body language and the body language of those around you. Did you change what you said or how you said it? Your Persona archetype might compel you to make changes to counter your desires. If you did make changes, ask yourself, "Why did I say it like that?" or "Why didn't I just say what I wanted to?" After you have chosen one of these possible activities during the day, you'll need to choose an activity for the night.

The exercise that you do at night or after work most likely will be an exercise that you believe will take more time. As a suggestion, you can do exercise number two, the exercise titled Now You. It could take more self-reflection than the others and, therefore, would be best done when you have some more time. Remember while you're doing these daily exercises that they can take a toll on your emotional batteries.

To recharge these emotional batteries, do a gratitude exercise every 2 to 3 days during this 21-day journey. Listed within the exercise choice section are a couple of gratitude exercise examples. Over your 21-day journey, you can alternate between the two or just choose one of them. There are no wrong answers; whatever you think will help you is a good choice.

Pass It Along

It may also be a good choice to pass this Shadow Workbook along to someone you know. Everyone has room for self-improvement, and if it helps you, you can help someone else too. Even if you just share the book with someone as a part of your journey, it's a good choice. Bringing others into the fold and endeavoring on this journey together can be very therapeutic. You can even share the Shadow Workbook with your partner after the 21 days or during the process.

Using the Workbook With a Partner

Talking to your partner about your journey, your exploration, and learning more about your inner child will allow you to do a deeper dive. Remember, the world around you affects your shadow self. When you have an intimate relationship, it's important to include those around you in your experiences. Start a conversation with your partner about what you learned about yourself and listen to any feedback they might have. Your partner could support you in your endeavors to eliminate your anxiety and negativity. One reason to include someone that cares about you is that having a support system will enable you to maximize your chances of success. Include your partner in the vision for your future, imagining your future self without anxiety and negativity. Approaching the Shadow Workbook in this way will allow you to gain all the benefits of this tool.

SHADOW PLAN EXERCISES

Keeping in mind the exercise examples that were given throughout the book, these are some daily exercises that you can do. They will help you eliminate your anxiety and negativity, plus they are easily integrated into your daily life.

Morning Exercise

The morning is a perfect time to reflect and analyze the shadow archetype. The Shadow archetype often comes out in dreams; when you wake up, reflect and analyze what you dreamt about. Try to remember what you were thinking about before you fell asleep. One technique you could do is, after waking up late, write how well you slept on a scale of one to ten. While you get ready in the morning, analyze the contents of your dreams, and think about what they might mean to you. Carl Jung believed that dreams were our brains' way of processing things that we were incapable of or not able to do during the day. Another morning exercise that you could do is make a mental list of everything that you want to get done, or a physical list if that helps. While making your mental or physical list think about the things that you desire out of that particular day. One thing that you could desire out of the day is to put some time aside for a fun activity. When you take time to do the things that you like, it can help contrast your anxiety and negativity.

When trying to eliminate your anxiety and negativity, another good morning activity to analyze your Shadow archetype is to think about the day before. You can analyze it and find where you came up short. The shortcomings associated with your Shadow archetype and the imbalance in this area are likely the cause of your negativity or anxiety. It's important when trying to make self-improvement to start the day off strong. It's also important to keep that energy going throughout the day, which is why it's crucial to plan an activity to do during the day.

During The Day

After you start your day, you need to keep that energy going, so here are a few ideas on activities that you can do throughout the day. The day is the best time to analyze your Persona and Anima archetypes because to analyze them you must observe your behavior or feelings with others. Like the trigger log, you need to observe how your behavior changes with others. It may influence our choice of words, tone of voice, and even posture. While you observe your possible behavioral changes, you will be collecting information about your Persona archetype. It's who we are with others, not one more alone, that is truly telling.

If you do change your behaviors drastically with others, it could be a source of your negativity and anxiety. It's not uncommon to change who we are to fit in, but it is crucial for our happiness not to. Once you get to know your inner child and your authentic self, it's important to show other people this part of yourself. When you can be confident with who you are as a person, there will be no need for anxiety or negativity.

If you find yourself saying different words than those you'd want to use, the first thing you need to do is figure out why. It could be that you're talking to your boss, you're trying to get more professional, or it could be that you're afraid of offending someone. When you're not saying what you want to the person you're talking to, they don't really know the real you. We instinctively want those around us to love us for us. The only way for those closest to you to get to know the real you is to be brave enough to show it to them. There is no need to hide your authentic self. Your self-reflection does not end when the sun goes down.

At Night

When your day is ending and the sun goes down, the last amount of analyzing for the day that needs to be done is about your Self archetype. You should do your nighttime exercise early enough to have time every three days to also do a gratitude exercise. At night, before the gratitude exercise, reflect on the day's events. You spent the day being aware and observant of your surroundings. Now the day is ending, and it's time to analyze that information further.

Try and remember how you felt and what made you feel that way. The Self archetype has a lot to do with the instincts you were born with and taught as a child. Your life now is very different from when you were two years old, but your instincts are not. When you feel anxious, but you don't know why, it's because your subconscious is telling you there's something wrong in your life. Was there something that happened during the day that made you feel bad? If your boss is telling you that you're not doing a good job or a friend is saying you're not being a good friend, there's only one thing to do. To make it better, you can either accept that they're right and do better or they're wrong, so you need to set them straight. It's the continued exposure to a negative environment that makes us negative.

To get rid of your negativity and anxiety, you must make some changes. Like the beginning of the day, the end of the day is the time to think about solutions and changes you can make. Unlike in the morning, now that the sun is going down, it's time to weed out the bad habits and bad influences. Anything in your life that can hurt you but not help you needs to go. Weeding out the negative in your life can be stressful, so make sure to do a gratitude exercise at the end of the day before you go to bed, every three days.

One gratitude exercise that you can do is to make a list of ten things you are grateful for. When you do it, you can stay positive about your life and, in turn, be motivated to make changes. You will hold on to that feeling of gratitude and recognize that by eliminating the negativity in your life, you can feel it more. Another gratitude exercise that you can do is list all the important people in your life that care about you. When you're feeling anxiety and negativity, it's easy to feel alone, but you're not.

It can be helpful to carry this list of people that support you to help motivate you through your 21-day journey. You will need to be moving forward to eliminate your anxiety and negativity every day, not just every three days; make sure to check off the days as you complete them on your Shadow Plan calendar. Doing that gives you a sense of accomplishment and affirms that you're putting in an effort. If you have a sense of accomplishment, even a small one, this will help you stay positive. The Shadow Plan calendar can also be used to mark the days that you are supposed to do gratitude exercises and in many other different ways to help you eliminate your anxiety.

The Shadow Plan calendar can be used like your everyday calendar, but there are ways to use it to make it more effective. These tips are quick and won't add any more undue stress upon you while you are on your journey. Remember that every ounce of effort you put into your self-improvement will get back tenfold later when you succeed.

One tip that will help with your self-improvement while using this calendar is changing the color of the pen or writing instrument that you use to cross off the day. Crossing off the days with a different color each day will help you better pass the time, because you won't be focusing on the days you have left. Each day you complete will be able to stand out as a day that you succeeded in your efforts to self-improve. Doing this tip and the following will help you stay positive, which is crucial to your elimination of negativity and anxiety.

Another helpful tip is placing a sticky note on top of your calendar with your goal written on it. You could write something like, "I will live life without anxiety and negativity." Reading this each day will help you focus on the future and not on how you passed a day that might have been hard.

Each day you will have to remove that sticking out and read your goal, which will help motivate you to keep going. Your sticky note might also say, "I made it through another day!" This statement reminds you of what you have accomplished so far and helps keep you positive for yet another day. You can also remind yourself of your accomplishments by showing your Workbook to a loved one.

Show your Workbook calendar with the cross-off days to a loved one so that you know that they know that you're completing each day. Having someone you know also know that you are making steps to improve your life reinforces the progress you are making. Carl Jung said that our environment plays a crucial role in our state of mind. Showing your workbook calendar to someone helps you create an environment with your loved ones where progress is being made.

There are other ways to use this Shadow Plan calendar to maximize your success, but these are just a few to get you started and help you make the calendar as effective as possible. However, feel free to brainstorm some others: this is your journey of self-improvement to eliminate your anxiety and negativity, so it must be customized for you. It's possible that seeing the days you have left becoming fewer and fewer will help you keep going. If you see that number getting smaller, it helps to use a black pen to cross out the days or shade the days in completely. Trying to eliminate your anxiety and negativity is inflamed by focusing on it.

If you need to try not to focus on it to continue your journey, don't put a sticky note on your calendar; it could do more harm than good. Maybe you're not ready to share your journey with others quite yet. While it's okay not to do it right now, it is important to share it with someone eventually. No one can help you if they don't know what you're going through.

Yes, there is a stigma with having anxiety and negativity, but those that care about you will understand. The people that really care about you will want to help you. Try accepting that you have these feelings and work towards sharing your struggle with someone that you care about, even if you can't right now.

CONCLUSION

To summarize, you are endeavoring to analyze your shadow self. While analyzing yourself, you will be reflecting and using the four main archetypes to get to know your inner child. You will identify your triggers and find their source. After finding the source, you will postulate solutions so that you may eliminate your negativity and anxiety.

By doing this, you will enable yourself to enjoy life to the fullest. After using the Shadow Workbook, you will live a life without anxiety and negativity consuming you. In this way, you can enjoy the moment and better participate in life. You are on an ongoing journey; therefore, explore the possibility of continuing to use these methods to explore your shadow self.

There will always be something new to learn about yourself since you are ever-changing. New situations will arise, and this Workbook will allow you to tackle each trigger as it occurs. With each layer of yourself that you explore, another will be underneath. You can exercise daily in the foreseeable future with the activities in this Shadow Workbook.

The meditation exercise can become a daily habit that you do every morning on the way to work. Even the trigger log can be used to identify problems that occur throughout the day. Keeping this trigger log will allow you to self-analyze and postulate other possible self-improvements. It could also be helpful to keep setting new and improved goals using the Dear Future Me exercise. As you complete goals, it is possible to keep setting new ones. There's no end to the self-improvement that you can do. It's only once you are happy and fully proud of yourself that you can stop. Anytime you identify a possible room for improvement, you can refer back to this Shadow Workbook to help you.

This is your Shadow Workbook to help you on your journey to self-improvement.

Take hold of this Workbook and begin the process of eliminating your anxiety and negativity.
Really commit fully to the next 21 days and unwaveringly get to know your authentic self. Set those goals! Achieve those goals! You will be better off using this Shadow Workbook!

SHADOW PLAN
CALENDAR

On the next page is the calendar that you can use to check off the days as you complete them.

You can write in the days or mark it with a symbol to indicate that you need to complete a gratitude exercise. You can enter the exercises you do day by day in the calendar to keep track of your entire journey. This calendar is the final tool afforded to you in this Shadow Workbook. Look back on the content and reread these pages if you feel it's necessary.

As you complete the 21 days to eliminate your anxiety and negativity, reflect on what you have learned in this Shadow Workbook and continue to do so if it helps.

Enjoy it!

DAY 1
_____
_____
_____

DAY 2
_____
_____
_____

DAY 3
_____
_____
_____

DAY 4
_____
_____
_____

DAY 5
_____
_____
_____

DAY 6
_____
_____
_____

DAY 7
_____
_____
_____

DAY 8
_____
_____
_____

DAY 9
_____
_____
_____

DAY 10
_____
_____
_____

DAY 11
_____
_____
_____

DAY 12
_____
_____
_____

DAY 13
_____
_____
_____

DAY 14
_____
_____
_____

DAY 15
_____
_____
_____

DAY 16
_____
_____
_____

DAY 17
_____
_____
_____

DAY 18
_____
_____
_____

DAY19
_____
_____
_____

DAY 20
_____
_____
_____

DAY 21
_____
_____
_____

A typical Shadow Day...

Morning

- Sleep rating
- Gratitude list
- Dream analysis

During the day

- Trigger log
- Archetypes problem analysis
- Mantras

Night

- Analysis of the day's events
- Daily changes you can make
- List of the good things you've done

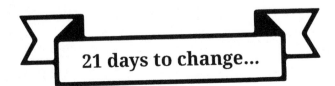

21 days to change...

EXERCISES
Sleep rating
Gratitude list
Dream analysis
Identifying Your Shadow
Trigger log
Who am I
Dear future me
Identifying Shadow Patterns in Relationships
Shadow Affirmations
Analysis of archetypes for a problem
Mantras
Working with Your Shadow
Identifying Inner Blocks
Facing your fears
A letter to little me
Mirror exercise
Meditation
Rewriting your thoughts
Reflecting of the day's events
Daily changes you can make
Plan the next day
List the good things you've done
Letter of Forgiveness
Thanks to the Others
Recognition of the Past
Breath and Relaxation
Visualization of the ideal future

Shadow work is a personal and transformative journey of self-exploration. The exercises in the table above offer a starting point to explore hidden aspects of yourself, confront suppressed emotions, and embrace your shadows. Remember that this process is subjective and unique for each individual. Feel free to reduce or add more exercises into the plan.

Congratulations on completing the Workbook and the 21-day shadow plan! This shows your dedication, commitment, and determination in achieving your goals and continuously improving. I am certain that this journey has provided you with new knowledge, skills, and opportunities that will be useful in the future.

Completing this program demonstrates that you are a person who does not give up in the face of challenges and you work hard to achieve your goals. I am proud of you and I am sure that your success will continue to grow.

The future is full of opportunities, and I am sure that you know how to seize every one of them to continue growing and improving. I encourage you to maintain the enthusiasm and dedication that you showed during the program and to continue pursuing your dreams. If you enjoyed this journey, don't stop here but continue with blocks, maybe 21 more days or even a 66-day calendar, to continue your work in discovering your shadow.

Good luck and have fun! Once again, congratulations on your success, and good luck in the future! I am sure that you will continue to achieve great things.

FREE SPACES

FREE SPACES

FREE SPACES

FREE SPACES

Your support is important to me!

Great things can start from a small gesture!

Leave a sincere review to support my work.

This would help to share and find this knowledge more easily to people who are looking for it.

REFERENCES QUOTES

Jung, C. G. " 'Modern Man in Search of a Soul', Ch. 11 pg 234-235, "We cannot change anything unless we accept it".

Jung, C. G. "knowing your own darkness is the best method for dealing with the darkness of other people. It's the confidence and self-assurance within ourselves that allows us to have the strength to deal with everyday life. While it's true the journey

Jung, C. G. "There's no coming to consciousness without pain.".

Jung, C. G. "I am not what happened to me; I am what I choose to become.".

Jung, C. G. "the most terrifying thing is to accept oneself completely.".

Jung, C. G. "There's no coming to conscious without pain."

Jung, C. G. "To confront a person with his shadow is to show him his own light."

REFERENCES

Erika Stoerkel. "The Science and Research on Gratitude and Happiness." PositivePsychology.com, June 23, 2022. https://positivepsychology.com/gratitude-happiness-research/#science-and-research.

John M. Grohol, Psy.D. "The Connection between Mental & Physical Health." Psych Central. Psych Central, February 25, 2009. https://psychcentral.com/blog/the-connection-between-mental-physical-health#1.

Kluger, Jeffrey. "Consciousness: It's Less than You Think." Time. Time, June 26, 2015. https://time.com/3937351/consciousness-unconsciousness-brain/.

"Mental Health Disorder Statistics." Johns Hopkins Medicine, November 19, 2019. https://www.hopkinsmedicine.org/health/wellness-and-prevention/mental-health-disorder-statistics.

Nattrauma. "Trauma Statistics & Facts." Coalition for National Trauma Research, December 21, 2021. https://www.nattrauma.org/trauma-statistics-facts/.

Othon, Jack E. "Carl Jung and the Shadow: The Ultimate Guide to the Human Dark Side." HighExistence, August 7, 2020. https://highexistence.com/carl-jung-shadow-guide-unconscious/.

"The Power of Positive Thinking." Johns Hopkins Medicine, November 1, 2021. https://www.hopkinsmedicine.org/health/wellness-and-prevention/the-power-of-positive-thinking.

"The Shadow." Society of Analytical Psychology, May 13, 2022. https://www.thesap.org.uk/articles-on-jungian-psychology-2/about-analysis-and-therapy/the-shadow/.

"A Showcase for the Mind-Body Connection." Monitor on Psychology. American Psychological Association. Accessed August 2, 2022. https://www.apa.org/monitor/sep05/showcase.

"Statistics for Mental Trauma: How Common Is IT & Who It Affects." FHE Health – Addiction & Mental Health Care. Accessed August 2, 2022. https://fherehab.com/trauma/statistics.

"What Is Gratitude? 5 Ways to Practice Being Thankful." What Is Gratitude? 5 Ways to Practice Being Thankful, April 30, 2021. https://www.betterup.com/blog/gratitude-definition-how-to-practice.

Made in the USA
Middletown, DE
26 September 2023

39466205R00097